THE
BEST FROM
OUT WEST

THE
BEST FROM
OUT WEST

·

Chuck Woodbury

WILLIAM MORROW AND COMPANY, INC.
NEW YORK

Recognizing the importance of preserving what has been written, it is
the policy of William Morrow and Company, Inc., and its imprints and
affiliates to have the books it publishes printed on acid-free paper,
and we exert our best efforts to that end.

Library of Congress Cataloging-in-Publication Data

Woodbury, Chuck.
    The best from Out West / Chuck Woodbury.
      p.   cm.
    ISBN 0-688-08588-1
    1. West (U.S.)—Description and travel—1981– 2. Woodbury, Charles M. Wood-
bury III
    —Journey—West (U.S.) I. Title.
    F595.3.W66   1990
    917.804'33—dc20

                                                                    89-78480
                                                                    CIP

Printed in the United States of America

First Edition

1 2 3 4 5 6 7 8 9 10

CONTENTS

INTRODUCTION

THIS book proves that dreams come true.

Beginning in the late 1970s, I dreamed of being a modern-day nomad—of traveling the back roads with no particular route or schedule. I could not look at a photo of a beautiful highway without feeling the urge to drive it. Charles Kuralt's "on-the-road" reports on CBS-TV drove me crazy. Willie Nelson's song "On the Road Again" was my anthem.

From 1978 to 1987, I plotted how I could live on the road. My main concern, of course, was how to support myself. A favorite plan was to write about what I found and sell the articles to magazines.

In 1982, on the way home from a dinner date, I spotted a used mini motor home with a FOR SALE sign in its window. A few days later, I emptied my savings account and bought it. I'll never forget the drive home. It was thrilling to look in my rearview mirror and see a little porta-home following along behind the driver's seat.

During the next few years, I took many one- and two-week trips to get a taste of life on the road. I wrote articles and took photos, but managed to earn only a few hundred dollars each trip. I would always have to return home to hustle some free-lance public relations work to pay my bills.

The nomadic life was both good and bad. Sometimes I was so happy I could hardly stand it; other times I was lonely and depressed. Nights in isolated campgrounds were the worst—with no one to talk with, no telephone to call friends, and no television to pass the time. Several times, I was ready to abandon my dream, go home, and get a job. Thankfully, I never did.

Gradually, though, I learned to cope with the isolation. And with each trip I fell more in love with the nomadic life—camping by a stream, eating greasy burgers in cafes named Eat, swapping tall tales with old men in seedy bars, and sitting by a campfire at night and watching the stars. And there were the roads themselves—straight ones, curvy ones, busy ones, lonely ones. But they were all good ones—pathways to points unknown.

Unfortunately, it was a life I could only afford to lead part-time. I was forced to spend 90 percent of my time in Sacramento doing public relations work to earn a living.

In 1984, the small country club community of Rancho Murieta, California, was looking for someone to publish its local newspaper. Although the thought of covering golf tournaments, the elementary school, and the Country Club Employee of the Month was not my idea of a dream assignment, the money was good—and at the time I needed it. The monthly schedule, too, allowed me to take some short trips. So it wasn't a bad way to earn a living—at least for a while.

For the next two years I was an unenthusiastic local newspaper publisher (and editor, advertising manager, etc.). I worked a lot, traveled a little, and saved my money. I also acquired a desktop publishing system—Macintosh computer and laser printer—the tools to publish. And all the while I dreamed of being a nomad.

By 1986, I was tired of writing about ladies' golf, tired of selling ads to beauty shops and financial planners, and at age thirty-nine I was on the verge of a midlife crisis. So I sold the *Murieta*

Times and hit the road. I took along the Macintosh and a portable photo darkroom so I could work along the way.

It was great! After a while, income from my writing was semi-respectable. Finding stories was no problem; if I pulled into a town and couldn't find something by nosing around, I'd search out a newspaper recycling bin, pull up beside it, brew a pot of coffee, arm myself with scissors, and then read newspapers. Within an hour I'd have two or three story leads.

But I kept thinking that I was wasting my desktop publishing system. Wasn't there a way to use it on the road?

Then, in October 1987, while driving along lonely Wyoming Highway 120, I had a brainstorm that would change my life. It was just like in the cartoons, when a light bulb goes off over a character's head. In my case, inside the little puffed cloud was an idea: *Publish a quarterly "on-the-road" newspaper.*

For the next few days I planned *Out West.* I would cover only eleven western states—a manageable beat for one person; I would take four six-week trips each year, writing at least two dozen articles each time out. I would then return to Sacramento, read my mail, paste up the issue, have it printed, then go back on the road. My motor home would be both my home and my newsroom on wheels.

One of my biggest decisions was not to accept advertising. Even though advertising revenue is the lifeblood of 99 percent of the consumer periodicals in America, I decided not to accept it. I had several reasons: First, I did not want to sell it myself; second, I could not afford to hire anybody; and third, I reasoned that most Americans were up to their eyeballs in advertising already. So I wouldn't add to the clutter.

I'd rely instead on subscriptions. I figured that with some luck I might break even in a few issues; maybe I could even earn a living off *Out West* someday.

Excited, I returned home and immediately pasted up a twenty-four-page tabloid newspaper, filling it with articles I had previously written for other periodicals. In late December, thirty-five hundred copies rolled off the press. I loaded the motor home with a couple thousand copies to give out as samples, and mailed five hundred copies to the media, hoping for a little free publicity. My entire investment, by the way, was less than a thousand dollars.

INTRODUCTION

What happened next astounded me. Reporters from newspapers, magazines, radio, and television called asking for interviews. Soon, my mailbox was stuffed with subscriptions. One day more than 140 arrived.

In April 1988, a four-man crew from *ABC World News Tonight* spent two days with me on the back roads of Nevada. I felt like a movie star. A few days later millions of people learned about *Out West*.

During the next year, *Out West* was also featured on CBS and NBC, by Associated Press, and by hundreds of newspapers and magazines, including the *Los Angeles Times, The Washington Post*, and *People* magazine. *Washington Journalism Review* featured me in its "Movers and Shakers" column. In my case, it was true in a literal sense.

All the while, I was spending half of my life on the road, and half at home, just as I had planned. My traveling office was the motor-home dinette or a picnic table, and my connection with the world the nearest phone booth. My telephone answering machine back in Sacramento relayed messages to me, and my sister Judi Hallbourg and her family picked up my mail and dealt with pressing matters.

As I traveled, I stopped by local newspapers, partly to socialize, partly to hustle some PR. Most of the newspapers would do an article; the result would be a surge in new subscriptions.

My friends asked me what it was like to experience such sudden success. I told them it was like being Walter Mitty and awakening to find my dreams had come true.

This book, much of it a collection from my "Roadside Journal" column, is part of that dream. I hope you enjoy it.

Chuck Woodbury
Sacramento, California

PROLOGUE

WHY is it, I wonder, that I love this road so? In my travels, I have seen a hundred such roads. I cannot be sure where I took this photo, but it doesn't matter; I love this road wherever it is.

When I am at home and stare at this photo, I want to be traveling. I want to explore. A feeling comes over me that maybe you have felt—the urge to be somewhere else—to be away from things familiar. Do you know that feeling?

If I were driving this road now, I would be trying to guess the distance to the mountains. Five miles? Ten miles? I would check my odometer, then check it again at the foot of the mountain. It's a game I once played to pass time, but I now play for fun.

This road would have bored me as a child. There is nothing much to see—just a long ribbon of asphalt that seems to extend forever into the desert. In my high school mechanical-drawing

class, I drew such roads at my drafting table. Maybe that is when my love affair with these roads began.

I have never understood this love. My guess is these roads are so different from city roads that they somehow refresh me. A busy city clogs my mind, and much of the reason is the stress of driving there—heavy traffic, frequent stoplights, and rude drivers. Driving a lonely road like this one cleanses my clogged mind. I feel refreshed, invigorated, and ready for anything.

Many times the traffic is so light you can stop in your lane for a ten-minute stretch without the approach of another car. Cows will stare at you, and you can stare back at them, and it will be just you and the cows and that's all.

At night, you may see only a distant light or two—a ranch or another vehicle. And above, a vast universe awaits your gaze. This is a road to drive on a warm summer night in a convertible.

Sadly, this road is a dinosaur. A multilane Interstate is much preferred by a society preoccupied with speed.

But I don't care, for I love this road anyway.

Why? I just do. That's reason enough.

THE
BEST FROM
OUT WEST

CHAPTER ONE

CALIFORNIA

Sometimes when I am working inside my motor home I feel like the Wizard of Oz. It has to do with working from a small space, and knowing nobody knows where I am.

Tonight all my window shades are pulled and my electric heater is keeping me toasty warm. I'm out of range of TV, and I don't feel like reading, so I am writing. I am a writer lost in America in a tiny tin cabin on wheels.

My home is tidy, except for one dirty pan on my stove; earlier it heated my dinner of tomato soup. A slice of apple pie is on the counter. In an hour I will feast on it, along with a freshly perked cup of coffee.

After that, I may step outside to visit my friends the stars. Or I may remain inside, and stretch by walking laps in my minihouse. Such a workout involves taking three steps in one direction and then three steps in the other direction and then repeating the process.

Perhaps the greatest thing about my portable home is that I associate it with so many wonderful adventures. We have been to thousands of towns and met hundreds of people together. Through its windows I have seen lakes and streams, mountain peaks, wheat fields, farms, and all sorts of animals—deer, moose, antelope, cows, squirrels.

Tomorrow I'll return the computer to its hiding spot, latch down the drawers and cupboards, and point my motorized home east.

This is the life.

If this sounds too perfect, be aware that it is not. Sometimes my life on the road is scary—yes, I said scary. You're probably wondering what I'm talking about, so I'll tell you of one of my worst fears. Now, if you think I'm talking about a nuclear holocaust, or of being smashed head-on by a logging truck, you are wrong.

What I fear most is losing my wallet down a pit toilet.

If you're laughing, please don't. Please understand that even admitting this fear to you is painful. The thought of losing my Visa card and driver's license down a dark and dreary hole in some national forest campground is nearly too much for this roving journalist to bear. When this thought strikes me—sometimes late at night when I'm half-asleep—it sends chills down my spine, pangs through my heart, and gas to my belly.

Do you have any idea of what I'm talking about? Do you?

The fear is rational. It could happen. So I am not wrong to be shaking in my boots at this very moment.

I ask you, what should I do if this really happens? Should I attempt to fetch my wallet? Could I capture it with a clothes hanger or would I have to climb down into the dark, slimy dungeon and probe by hand? Where would I enter? Would a flashlight illuminate my way? How deep would I have to search? How would I smell later?

Would I find my wallet? Maybe. Maybe not.

Would wading through the murkiest murk in the known universe be worth it? And really, should I even take on this foul task to simply rescue a replaceable Visa card, replaceable driver's license, replaceable ATM card, and thirty or forty bucks?

Do you think I would do that? I would not. I am so scared thinking about this that I must stop writing.

But speaking of pit toilets, I must bring up a problem that has bothered me for a long time. I don't know what can be done about it—maybe you'll have an idea. I wouldn't even bring it up, but I feel someone has to, and it might as well be me.

What I am talking about is the problem of mosquitoes that hide in the pits of pit toilets. I'm concerned about how we can get them out of there and up into the air where we can battle them with Raid, or swat them with newspaper inserts.

While I don't generally believe that one mosquito is smarter than the next, I am convinced that the inhabitants of the pits are of a superior intelligence. Somehow they know they have a vulnerable target—if only for a few moments.

What bothers me so much about this is that a creature no bigger than a pinhead can attack me at a time when I am so helpless. I know full well how to deal with a mosquito on a wall or ceiling, but when one hides so cleverly it has an unfair advantage. It makes me mad!

I hereby call for a public forum on this issue. We must rid the pits of mosquitoes. Write to your congressman. Write to Bush. Write to your mother, for Pete's sake! Just write. This is important.

Spiders, on the other hand, are a different matter. I don't mind them in outhouses. To a spider, the interior of a campground outhouse is a heaven on Earth. Flies and other assorted winged creatures fly inside these aromatic places by the hundreds to be snagged in carefully strung webs. It is a smorgasbord of enormous proportions to a spider—an earthly paradise where you just hang around and the food comes to you.

When I call my answering machine back home, I almost never think about what I'm accomplishing. A few minutes ago I did. I realized that by simply pushing some buttons, I could make a phone ring and then answer miles away.

I understand the answering machine, but I don't understand

how a phone can work so well. I know there are phone wires strung up all over the place, and my voice somehow goes through those, but I can't figure how it actually happens, much less how it does it so fast.

Radio amazes me even more. How can a little box reproduce music that somebody is playing miles away? I know the radio station sends out a signal that my radio receives, but that's about all I can figure out.

Sometimes I think about those signals. I know they are there, even though I don't see them. For example, at this very moment there are probably hundreds of them all around me. They're bumping against my body, bouncing off the sides of the motor home, and even inside my carton of milk in the refrigerator. At night, they sleep with me—under the covers and on top of the pillow.

Television is even more amazing than radio. My box with a screen not only reproduces sounds from somewhere else, but it also reproduces a moving picture. How can that be? With my brain operating at full capacity, I can't figure out how Johnny Carson gets inside that box.

Computers, of course, are also impossible to understand. How can so many words be stored on a memory chip smaller than a penny?

Devices I *can* understand are fans, blow dryers, shavers, flashlights, and Mr. Coffee machines.

People have asked me why I don't name my motor home. I don't know. I guess I just haven't been able to come up with a good name. Everything sounds corny. And personally, it seems silly to me to give a hunk of metal a name. I could call it Ralph or Mary or Steve or Fido or Juliette or even Bluto, but none of those names do anything for me. So my motor home is nameless, which is fine with me.

After visiting several thousand small towns in the West, I have come to understand them a bit. People sometimes ask me to define a small town. I used to stumble over this question, so one day I made a list of definitions. At the top of the list was: In a small town there is no McDonald's restaurant.

Here are some other ways to determine a small town:

- There are no stoplights.
- Residents know their neighbors.
- The movie theater has one screen.
- There's always a sleeping dog in front of the market.
- Markets don't have quick checkout lines.
- Main Street is still the main street.
- The bank has human tellers, not machines.
- Gas stations still do repair work, and gas costs the same whether you pay with cash or credit card.
- People know their auto mechanic.
- Restaurant bathrooms don't play Muzak.
- The Western Auto store is a big-time business.
- There are no elevators.
- The library can't afford a photocopy machine.
- The mail only goes out once a day, and everybody knows what time.
- There are no lines at the post office.
- The biggest celebrity is the quarterback of the high school football team.
- Everybody knows the mayor.
- The police chief has a pot-belly.
- The best place to get news is at the cafe.
- The surnames in the phone book are the same ones on the cemetery headstones.
- The best magazine rack is at the drug store.
- Eight out of ten waitresses chew gum.
- Push-button telephones aren't available yet.
- Hamburgers are still called hamburgers at the drive-in.
- People use CBs, not cellular phones.
- Kids still go to public schools.
- The best car is a pickup truck.

I've thought of getting a dog. A single man traveling alone—no matter how wholesome he looks (and I am a wholesome-looking fellow, I assure you)—is often viewed suspiciously. We live in a couple-oriented society, and single people are considered a little odd to begin with, except, of course, by other single people.

And there are a lot of weird and even dangerous people wandering around America. It's sad, but that's a fact. Single guys, and

21

groups of guys, are the most suspicious, even if they have the best intentions. But a guy with a dog—especially a small dog—is thought to be all right, unless, of course, his dog is a pit bull. In that case, there is a question of which would be the most threatening, the man or the pit bull.

So I might get a dog one of these days. But when I think about it, I already have some of the benefits of a pet without the hassles. Already today, I have visited with a roadrunner and several cottontail rabbits. Not bad, considering it's only eleven in the morning.

On some trips, my friends are chipmunks and squirrels. Other times they are comical bluejays. I have had near-encounters with moose and have petted a few deer, even though I shouldn't have. I have watched baby ducks walk alongside a road, and have thrown bread crumbs to their moms and dads. I have had minibattles with ornery geese, and have played a form of hide-and-seek with prairie dogs.

Of course, none of these creatures can substitute for a pet dog or cat. But, if you're not into Kitty Litter or pooper scoopers, they're a fair substitute.

I have also watched sparrows and robins and ravens and buzzards. Last evening, a small gray bird sat atop a Joshua tree and watched me for a few minutes. I stared back, smiling at his curious nature.

Looking into a cow's blank stare is a reminder of the comparative brilliance of humans. A friend once told me that cows have personalities. While I have not observed this personally, I have nevertheless spent a few enjoyable moments with these animals.

Cows are not smart. Still, I wonder what they think about as they look at you with their blank stares. They hardly ever change their expression. When you approach a cow, it will stare at you for a moment. Now at this point, a cow is doing some thinking. It is trying to decide if it should stay where it is or if it should run away. This may seem like a relatively easy decision for you or me, but for a big animal with the intelligence of a little gopher snake, this is a hard job. What the cow is doing is ascertaining the danger.

Cows, though, don't consciously ascertain. Since they don't speak, they can't think in actual words, as we do. I can't imagine what it would be like to be as stupid as a cow. If they measured a cow's IQ, I bet it would be 1 or 2.

Yet, this is good. A cow—if it knew it would one day be made into thousands of Whoppers—would be very depressed. A milk cow, knowing that she would be grabbed and sucked by a machine for all her productive life, would likely be despondent, perhaps even suicidal.

Sometimes when driving through farmland, I try to think what it would be like to be in a cow's place. If it is a beautiful spring day, it might be OK. But on a cold winter day, I would never want to be a cow.

I would especially not want to be a cow in a stockyard. You see these when you drive on Interstate 5 through central California. There are thousands of cows in each stockyard, usually in pens with foundations of equal parts of dirt, manure, and water. It's a muddy, awful mess—a gooey hell. Yet the poor cows, with nowhere to go, have to lie down in this slop. This, perhaps more than any other time, is when a cow is lucky to be so dumb.

I have a routine each morning that starts with the complicated process of getting out of bed. I must climb down from my upstairs bunk, using a short aluminum ladder. It's not as easy as getting out of bed at home, where I can basically roll out. If I roll out of my porta-home bed, I will fall four feet. So it usually takes me from fifteen minutes to a half hour to actually decide to get up. If it's cold, then it may take longer, for I'll be tempted to remain under my warm blankets.

After I finally arise, I turn on the heater if it's cold. If it's warm, I go to my next step, which is to prepare coffee. My coffeepot is the old-fashioned kind that heats on the stove and makes six cups, which will usually last me all day.

After starting the coffee, I get dressed and walk outside to light the hot-water heater; it takes about fifteen minutes for the five-gallon tank to heat. While it does, I go back inside to eat some cereal, read a newspaper from the day before, and drink my first cup of coffee.

Then it's time for my shower. My actual bathroom is about four square feet. It's basically a fold-up toilet in a shower stall, so

I fold up the toilet and prepare to bathe. I love this little shower, especially when I'm in the middle of a parking lot. I think: *Here I am in a K Mart parking lot and nobody knows that I am taking a shower.* Why that impresses me so, I don't know. It just does.

After my shower I get dressed. Then I must make an important decision: Do I stay camped where I am or do I move on? If I decide to stay, then I go for a walk, go fishing, or take my portable computer out to the picnic table to write. Some days, I read. If I decide to move on, then I must put everything in its place, secure the door and windows, and then find an interesting road.

Although I look at a map before leaving, I put it away and follow whatever pathway seems promising. Sometimes these routes dead-end, but most often they lead to an appealing town, and then to another road. Usually within a few hours I will find a story. Often I will meet an interesting person and end up camping in his or her backyard. If not, by late afternoon I start searching for a campsite. Usually I'll find one within a couple of hours. Then I settle in for the evening, often writing well into the night before going to sleep. Then the process starts over again.

I'm camped in Anza-Borrego State Park in southern California, and thankfully, the sun has set behind the nearby mountains. The temperature has dropped from 90 to 80 degrees. It's a perfect time to wash my clothes.

It's hot; there's a water faucet near my campsite, and there are no other campers to offend with my hung-out underwear. As I sit at my picnic table, the sight of my campsite makes me laugh. Underwear, towels, and T-shirts are strung up on the motor home's side mirrors, on the Yamahopper, and on bushes with branches strong enough to support wet laundry. I hope nobody drives by. The scene is tacky.

There are many things you may have in your kitchen that I don't have in my portable house. I don't have a microwave oven, an electric drip coffee maker, electric frying pan, electric can opener, food processor, or electric knife. My kitchen knife is an old-fashioned one with a blade that isn't plugged into anything. It works fine and provides hand exercise as a bonus.

Instead of a microwave oven, I have an old-fashioned gas oven, with a dial for setting the temperature. It takes a long time for baked potatoes to cook in it, so I don't cook them—instead, I make french fries on the stove top. When I'm on the road, french fries taste better anyway.

I don't have a cupboardful of plates or a drawerful of knives and forks. I have two plates although I use only one unless I have a guest. I have perhaps four or five knives and forks, although I use only a couple.

My can opener is one of those little gizmos that you turn in your hand. I've met people who can't operate one of these.

I have an old red coffeepot that I heat on my stove. When the water boils, the grinds perk and soon I have coffee. It's more work than my Mr. Coffee at home, but the taste is as good.

Despite my lack of modern conveniences, I am as much at home in my motor home as I am in my "real" home in Sacramento.

Here are a few other things I take along on my trips:

• My Walkman stereo. I load a tape, put on the headphones and enjoy stereo sound as good as from my home stereo. One of my favorite times to listen is at night. I take a pillow outside and lie on my back on a picnic table—taking in the music and the stars at the same time. I can't do that at home.
• My two televisions. My "big" set is a five-inch black-and-white model that runs on twelve-volt power. The other is a Sony Watchman, a two-inch TV that fits in my pocket. I often use this set to listen to the news, sometimes outside in my lawn chair.
• My CB. This is my telephone. Mostly I talk to truckers.
• My portable radio that receives AM, FM, and shortwave. Sometimes the only broadcasts I can receive are airline pilots talking to airport towers hundreds of miles away.
• My two computers. The Macintosh, of course, is the work-horse, but it needs household current. So when I'm in a camp-ground without 110 power, I use my battery-powered NEC.

I also carry a few things—"just in case":

• A sport jacket, just in case I'll need to get dressed up.

• A toolkit full of tools I'll never use, but I bring them along—just in case.

• A pair of good shoes—just in case I need to go to a formal event. (I never do.)

• Three or four cans of tuna, even though I use only about one can a year. A person never knows when he'll need tunafish.

I suspect about half of what I bring with me is "just in case" stuff. Someday it'll come in handy.

When I was writing earlier about my televisions, I forgot to mention how I sometimes watch my tiny Watchman TV on the tops of mountains.

Campgrounds are often in remote areas with lousy TV reception. So if I want to watch television, I have to find a better spot. What I sometimes do is carry my Watchman up a mountainside until I pick up a signal. Very often, of course, one never materializes—in which case I'm disappointed to miss the show, but happy to get some exercise.

A couple of years ago I climbed a mountain to watch a baseball playoff game. I was probably the only person for a hundred miles around watching a two-inch TV on a mountain peak.

There is something we say that's a lie, but we don't think of it that way. We tell it when somebody we don't know very well stops by our house. The minute they pass through the front door, we say, "Please excuse my messy house." We then explain how busy we've been with work, or with the kids, or that our in-laws just left—something like that. The idea, of course, is to convince the person that our house is normally cleaner—which, of course, it seldom is.

Thus, anticipating a visit, we spend an hour cleaning our place to make it look about as clean as it ever is except for wedding receptions or visits from Mother. We do the dishes, clean the toilet, hide dirty clothes in a closet (my favorite method of cleaning), dust the coffee table, and perhaps even vacuum the rug.

Convinced the place looks presentable, we wipe the sweat from our forehead, then wait for our visitor. Ten minutes later the doorbell rings.

We walk to the door, open it, smile, say hello, and then as we walk inside turn to the visitor and say, "Oh, please excuse my messy house."

The third-largest city in California has no traffic jams. It's not San Francisco, San Jose, or San Diego. It's California City, at 186.5 square miles, the third-largest city—in size, not in population. In area it's smaller than San Diego or Los Angeles, but nearly four times the size of San Francisco.

California City, founded in 1965, is near Edwards Air Force Base in the southern California desert. Most residents are retired folks, or workers who commute to the base. The population is only 5,015—an average of 27 people per square mile. That compares with 6,380 people per square mile in Los Angeles.

I stopped by the chamber of commerce to ask if any famous people lived in California City. The clerk thought for a minute, then said there was "a black guy who used to sing in a band." He lives in a mobile home but she didn't know where. I asked her if there was anybody else who was famous. She shook her head and said she couldn't think of anybody.

Earlier I wrote about how we often say "please excuse our messy house," even when our house isn't messy at all. It occurs to me that we say the same thing about our coffee. This morning I offered a couple of visiting journalists a cup of coffee. "Please excuse this stuff," I said. "It's the first pot I've made on this trip."

Truth be known, it tasted like every other cup of coffee I've ever made. In other words, not great, but not bad. Still, I felt that by giving this warning, if the fellows thought it was terrible, they would remember my words and think I was just out of practice.

Looking over Lake Cuyamaca makes me sad. It's beautiful here—rolling hills of golden grass, pine forest, and a deep-blue lake. But a cloud of smog is rolling in from the west.

I'm in the mountains forty miles east of San Diego. For the past week, I have been in southern California; smog has followed me much of the time.

The sadness I feel is because I remember southern California when the air was clean. I grew up near Los Angeles in West Covina. My family moved there in 1948, when it was mostly orange groves and a few thousand people. As a child, I played hide-and-seek in orange groves and chased jackrabbits in the San Juan Hills. Two-lane Garvey Boulevard and the Pacific Electric trolley line connected West Covina with the big city of Los Angeles.

When my family moved away in 1964, West Covina's population was sixty thousand. A village with orange groves had become a city of franchised food places. The general store had turned into a dozen shopping malls. The once-clear air was choked with the wastes from industry and a few million automobiles.

Today, camped near my childhood home, I am reminded that the smog still remains. Of course, I write now from my motor home, which spews filth from its exhaust pipe and thus contributes to the mess. So who am I to complain?

I'm frustrated. How can a person who has breathed the clear, sweet air of Nevada, Montana, or southern Utah not be saddened by this ugly sky?

What's my point? I'm upset that it's come to this—a huge, nature-blessed region so crammed with people and their pollution that the beauty of a mountain lake is ruined by an unhealthful cloud of weightless slop.

We've got to invent an automobile engine that doesn't pollute. With all our brilliant minds, somebody should be able to come up with one to do the job.

Here's something that doesn't happen very often. I was making a phone call this afternoon from a booth overlooking Lake Cuyamaca. It was an important call, and I wanted to be at my best.

The problem was that someone had cleaned some fish in the fish-cleaning sink nearby, and the guts were stinking up everything downwind, including my phone booth. It was as if the odor blew into the booth, then couldn't figure out how to get out. So it just hung around. Talk about house-a-tosis!

At home, the sounds of my life are usually the same: the noisy garbage truck on Tuesday morning; a car racing down J Street on Saturday night; a barking dog; the neighbor's stereo turned up too high; or the siren of a police car.

On the road, the sounds are less predictable. Right now, for example, a swarm of tiny flies is banging against my rear window, sounding very much like raindrops.

This morning, a woodpecker or its relative was pecking against the roof, making a terrible racket.

Often, there's the pleasing sound of a stream. Now, there is only the howl of the warm desert wind.

Tonight, in bed, I may hear the cries of coyotes. That's a sound I don't hear in Sacramento.

Sometimes there is no sound at all, a special treat.

It is a quiet morning here at Black Rock Canyon Campground in Joshua Tree National Monument. About an hour ago, I had my first cup of coffee in the company of a friendly roadrunner who was perched on my picnic table seeking food. I chose not to accommodate the creature, but it took him five minutes to figure that out; he just waited patiently for a morsel. I spoke to him, but he didn't react. He was more interested in food than talk. He slapped his beak together a few times to make a clapping sound, then he barked like a dog. He never once went *beep, beep,* which was a disappointment.

He finally figured out he wasn't going to get fed, so he left. He was in for a big surprise, because the nearest camper was a quarter mile away. But I guess if you're a roadrunner, the walk does you good.

According to the Joshua Tree Journal, a rattlesnake feeds once every ten to sixteen days. What does it do between meals?

Now you take a cow or horse or deer or even a bird—they are always eating. Have you ever seen a cow lounging around, just passing the time? No. When they aren't sleeping, they're eating. Same with a horse.

So what does a rattlesnake do with all its spare time? Does it just wait for the urge to eat? Does it meander around checking out the sights? Rattlesnakes aren't out hustling a date. I don't think they mate very much. Even when they do, it probably doesn't take long, except on a cold day. To be honest, I can't figure out how a snake mates anyway.

I wonder what those reptiles do all day?

*   *   *

Death Valley is one of my favorite places. Perhaps it has something to do with being in the middle of nowhere. I like the name Death Valley, and the other place names in Death Valley National Monument: Hells Gate, Dry Bone Canyon, Stovepipe Wells, Furnace Creek, Blackwater Gulch, Badwater, Coffin Peak, and Devils Cornfield.

A park ranger told some visitors yesterday that she works in Death Valley because "a test I took in high school told me I should be either a park ranger or a mortician. So I ended up as a park ranger in *Death Valley.*"

Park rangers report that the architects who designed the National Monument Visitor's Center purposely designed the theater in the shape of a coffin.

Strangely, though, it's said that only one person actually died in Death Valley before it was named. Apparently, the fellow was already sick when he arrived. So maybe Death Valley should be called Hot Valley. That would be appropriate. On July 10, 1913, the temperature in Death Valley reached 134 degrees. A spot in Libya reached 136 degrees once, but Death Valley has the consistently highest temperatures in the world. In the summer, the ground temperature can exceed 200 degrees. Try walking on that in your bare feet.

To illustrate how hot it gets in Death Valley, here's a story a park ranger told me: "Visitors come up to me and say it's not so hot here. They say where they live they can put a frying pan out in the sun on a hot summer day, crack an egg, and fry it right up. Well, I explain that we can do the same thing here, only we can do it in the shade."

Some people don't realize that Death Valley is in California. It doesn't seem to fit into a state known for smog, cellular telephones, beaches, and traffic jams. This morning I phoned a man in Toronto, Canada. He asked me where I was calling from, and I said Death Valley. "That's in Utah, isn't it?" I told him no.

"Gee," he said, "I always think of the big salt lake there in Utah and imagine Death Valley being somewhere around there."

Out my back window, a hundred RVs are parked side by side. I am a youngster here at the Sunset Campground at Furnace Creek

Ranch in Death Valley. The average age of these campers must be sixty.

One of the more interesting activities here is spying on people as they go about their everyday lives—lives usually hidden inside houses or behind fences. Here, much of what everybody does is in public view.

A woman in a blue sweater is standing on a stepladder washing the rear of her motor home as her husband observes from a few feet away. At the motor home next door, a woman is putting an athletic bandage on her knee. A few yards away, an older fellow in a yellow cowboy hat is sipping his morning coffee in a webbed lawn chair.

A woman just slammed the door of her RV with her arm instead of her hand. Her hand looked disfigured. I watched as she and her husband walked away and I wondered what their lives were like. For the day or two that we are parked here, the paths of our lives will cross. We will observe one another and make mental notes about what we see. I wonder how they see me—a lone man in a campground. They probably find me a curiosity.

I'm not sure why I'm so fascinated with a man putting up his TV antenna, or another fellow fumbling around his toolbox. I watched the woman wrap the athletic bandage around her knee as if it were a Hollywood movie; maybe it's because there was nothing much else to watch.

Just this very minute, a woman in ugly green pants slipped and nearly fell as she walked by. It was no big deal, and she didn't think twice about the episode. To me, it was entertainment.

An RVer couple down the campground from me in a beat-up old van are dead ringers for Ma and Pa Kettle. They have their cat leashed up outside the side door, and the feline is not happy. A cat, I think, resents a leash more than a dog does. For a cat to be happy, it must be free. Sometimes, I think I'm part cat.

A poodle barks from the motor home to my left; a man directly behind me hauls a water container to his travel trailer. A couple is walking toward the park bulletin board, carrying a paper plate with a message directing another RVer to their campsite. The people here are the lucky ones of their age group. They have the time and money to travel. Although a few of their mini porta-homes are old and ragged, most are new or fairly new and outfitted with the latest

31

conveniences: TVs, microwave ovens, and generators for power.

Many RVers carry along a piece of Astroturf for outside their front doors—sort of a portable, easy-care front lawn. Last evening, generators hummed from all directions—providing power for microwave-cooked dinners and *World News Tonight* with Peter Jennings.

My parents share my love for Death Valley, and usually visit at least once a year in their motor home. This year we ended up here together, which is terrific for me because I get some home-cooked meals (motor-home–cooked, actually).

This morning, my father and I walked from Furnace Creek Ranch to the Harmony Borax Works, about a mile away. We took a cross-country route, walking over powdery dirt and past mesquite, creosote, and desert holly bushes. We stopped for a few minutes to watch a lone coyote walk unhurriedly up a nearby hill. When it got to the top, it stood there in a classic coyote pose and surveyed the countryside, including us.

When we got to Harmony Borax Works, a young couple was taking turns photographing each other. My father asked them if they would like him to take their photo together. "Really? Are you serious?" the girl asked, as if it were a big chore. My dad said sure, so they handed him their camera, posed, and my father snapped their picture. They were all smiles as they walked away.

A few minutes later, an older fellow was getting ready to take a photo of his wife. Dad asked them if they would like their picture taken together, and they said they'd like that, so he took their photo. Mother told me later that my father does this wherever they go.

I have just smelled something terrific. It was the wonderful smell that comes when you open a coffee can and the pressurized air escapes sending the coffee aroma right up into your nose. The smell is better than the taste of the coffee.

But nearly as good as the smell is the coffee can itself. It can be used as a flowerpot, or for storing paper clips, rubber bands, pens, or pencils. Cheerios can be kept in an old coffee can. The can's plastic top holds the freshness in better than any cardboard box.

Yet, as handy as a coffee can is, I suspect it is headed the way of the reusable glass jar, into extinction. Something so good can't last in America these days when something lousy and useless will do the job half as well.

I visited the Roy Rogers and Dale Evans Museum in Victorville today. I hadn't been there for five years. The best exhibit was Trigger, the horse Roy rode in 188 films. He's stuffed, and in a big glass display case next to Buttermilk (Dale's horse) and Bullet (Roy's late dog).

Trigger hasn't changed since I last visited the museum, and that bothers me, because I have. I have more wrinkles, more gray hairs, and a slightly larger waistline. It doesn't seem fair that Trigger ages so well.

An argument can be made that I am better off than Trigger because Trigger is dead and I'm not. There is a lot to be said for being able to wake up each morning and go to bed each night, and watch *Action News* in between.

I wonder what Roy thinks when he looks at his stuffed horse, Trigger. Is it a good feeling? Does it make him happy or sad? At night, when the museum doors are locked, does Roy talk to his old friend about the great rides they shared? My guess is that looking at, touching, or talking to a stuffed horse—or any other stuffed former pet—is not satisfying. It's probably like talking to a photo. Trigger, I suspect, is there for the people who knew him only in films. To them, seeing him in the flesh—or hide, as in this case—is probably an exciting experience. It is to me, anyway.

This is a great museum if you're a movie buff. There are so many black-and-white pictures of Roy and Dale, you'd think they never did anything but pose. Two things I learned were that Roy's first job was in a shoe shop, and that Dale is Roy's second wife.

A thought struck me at the museum, and I want to share it with you, even though perhaps I shouldn't. It's just that I could not look at the stuffed Trigger, Buttermilk, and Bullet and not wonder where Roy and Dale will end up one day. I know this is an awful thought. I'm sorry. But it popped into my head all by itself even though I tried to keep it out. I really don't think I'm the first person to think it.

Victorville is a good-size town, so I decided to shop. What I needed most was a small generator for the motor home. Costco, a huge white store visible from the Interstate, looked like a good place. The reason, of course, is that generally speaking, the bigger the store, the lower the price. So I checked it out. But right inside the door, a woman stopped me and asked to see my membership card. I told her I had no membership card, but was interested in buying a generator so I could have some extra power for my little motor home which, it just so happened, was in the Costco parking lot at that very moment.

Well, she pointed to a spot about twenty-five yards away, where many people were standing in a long line. She told me I couldn't shop at Costco unless I was a Costco member. "But you can go over to that counter to see *if you qualify* for a one-day pass," she explained.

I looked at the line, and I asked myself what if I went over there and waited ten minutes to answer some questions and then failed to qualify for a one-day Costco membership? I figured I would have wasted a lot of time, and I might even be embarrassed. I was not about to be embarrassed, and I couldn't afford to waste any time because my schedule was quite busy: an appointment in Vegas in a week, another issue to put out in two months, and *Wheel of Fortune* was due on the telly in three hours. So, very politely, I told the woman that I wouldn't be shopping at Costco. I told her I was a very busy man and didn't have time to wait in line. She seemed to accept what I said, even though I sensed she might be thinking there was something odd about a guy who would turn down the opportunity to qualify for a one-day membership at Costco.

As I walked away, I thought that Costco might have milked a few hundred bucks from me if they had only played their cards right. Their mistake, I figured, was requiring me to qualify for a one-day pass, a costly marketing error in this particular instance.

So I went next door to Home Club, which let me in without a membership card, although it charges nonmembers an extra 5 percent. This store, all by itself, was bigger than most of the towns I'd visited in Nevada. There were so many shelves, and they were so high, that my mind was all boggled up. After a week of shopping at the general store in Death Valley, this was like going from a rowboat to a battleship. I'm not sure, but I think there were in the neighborhood of ten thousand checkout lines.

One row of merchandise was all toilets—from basic to fancy,

cheap to expensive. But there were none of the pit variety—a model dear to those of us who spend megahours in Forest Service campgrounds. And how about those toilet seats! There were more than I normally see in a couple of years. And the colors! Every color of the rainbow was represented on those seats, some of which were padded!

But they only had a few generators and they were too big for me. So, tired and disappointed, I left in search of a campground.

Shopping is hell.

I talked with a few people today here in Victorville. They told me that the reason this Mojave Desert community is growing so fast is that people live here and commute to work in Los Angeles. "It can take as long as three and a half hours some days," one man said, and he meant *one way*. A fast trip is at least two hours.

The reason they put up with the long commute is that homes here cost about half what they do in Los Angeles.

Still, why would anybody spend five to seven hours a day driving to and from work? I'm trying to answer that question but my brain keeps saying, "does not compute, does not compute."

Actually, I have wondered for years if commuting on clogged freeways isn't one of the most stressful things we do. I noticed one day, while driving in rush-hour traffic, that my hands were gripping the steering wheel very tightly. I was all tensed-up and that tenseness was showing up in my hands.

Speaking of traffic, I was parked the other night outside the Amargosa Opera House in Death Valley Junction (population, four), waiting for the doors to open for Marta Becket's one-woman show. She's performed thousands of times since she arrived at Death Valley Junction in 1967; I decided it was time to see her in action. Anyway, I had a half hour to wait, so I holed-up in the warm motor home, listening to KNX radio from Los Angeles. The air-watch reporter was telling of traffic jams on the Santa Monica Freeway and the San Bernardino Freeway, and on other freeways, and it seemed to me that I must be in a different world.

I wanted to call KNX and tell the reporter that in the last fifteen minutes, only one car had passed through Death Valley Junction.

By the way, Marta Becket's show was terrific. On her desert

35

stage she performs classical ballet, mime, and old-fashioned melodrama. Becket and her Opera House are amazing and wonderful.

We Americans, especially westerners, love our cars and will do almost anything to avoid taking public transportation. We will sit hour after hour in our cars on a clogged freeway in order to avoid taking a bus.

In my hometown of Sacramento, traffic engineers say that *no matter what they do*—build more freeways, build more light-rail track, add more buses—the traffic problem will get *worse* in the years ahead! Cities like Los Angeles, New York, Denver, Seattle, and dozens of other towns already have monumental traffic jams. And just think: People who commute three hours a day spend more than a month each year behind the wheel! Think of all the time they waste, not to mention gas.

We must do something. Some innovative city planners are suggesting minicities with clusters of homes and offices in the same area. People can commute to work by walking, riding bicycles, or local public transit. Employers should encourage employees to work at home. Fax machines and computers with modems make it possible; more and more people are working this way all the time, but more could be doing it. We must get off the road in really huge numbers. If we do, our air will be cleaner, and we'll still have gasoline for taking weekend trips and vacations.

A Lincoln Continental was tailgating me earlier. A clown was at the wheel, a red-haired fellow with madeup face, red nose—the works. He was staring straight ahead, leaning slightly forward, like drivers do when they're in a hurry. I was going fifty in a forty zone, but the clown wanted to go even faster. He was a weird sight in my rearview mirror.

There seems to be a rule about a construction zone with a traffic delay. It goes like this: When you approach a flagger-person with a stop sign, you arrive just in time to miss the line of traffic being allowed to pass through. So, you will have to wait. You will almost never arrive just in time to pass through with the traffic.

Speed-limit signs in highway construction zones often don't make sense. Speed limits are sometimes as low as twenty-five miles an hour, yet most cars move along at forty-five to fifty-five. If you go twenty-five, you'll be honked at, screamed at, and hated.

Around corners on some back roads, signs often warn to slow down to fifteen or twenty-five miles per hour. Even in my motor home, I can easily take most of these curves faster than that. Sports cars often don't even have to slow down at all. The oddest signs are the ones in fifty-five-mile zones that say to SLOW TO 55. Either the signs are leftovers from the sixty-five-limit days, or the highway people figure most motorists are speeding anyway, so fifty-five is really a slower speed.

Another sign that doesn't necessarily mean anything is ROUGH ROAD. Only about 20 percent of the time is the road actually rough. Most of the time, there's only a chuck hole or two—but there are many of those in places without warning signs. BUMP signs are also hard to figure. Sometimes you see the sign, then you wait for a bump, and you wait some more, and you never bump. In other places, there are plenty of bumps, but no signs.

Here's a driving tip for you: Never follow a gravel truck or a cattle truck. The first may harm your windshield and the second may harm your nose.

It's interesting how your mind works when you're driving a lonely road. Ideas pop in from every direction. Crazy ideas. I guess it's because your mind has time to ponder.

One time, driving from Salt Lake City to Sacramento on Interstate 80, I thought all the way about opening a restaurant that sold burritos. I figured employees could dress up in Superman-type costumes. The restaurant would be named Super Burrito. For six hundred miles, I planned how I would sell burritos in a Superman cape. One hundred miles from home, I knew I would soon be rich. I couldn't wait to tell my friends.

I awoke the next morning refreshed from a good night's sleep. I thought of my new business for perhaps two minutes. But at the start of minute three, I realized something: My idea was terrible. So much for Super Burrito.

Today, an idea of a different kind popped into my head. It came about after traveling a road with many dips. It was a boring road in the desert—a minor highway with chuck holes, patched pavement, and dips.

37

My mind was apparently thinking a lot about those dips, even though it didn't consciously let me know. While I wasn't paying particular attention to the dark spots at the bottom of each dip—the places where many cars dripped oil as they passed—my subconscious mind was. After passing over perhaps a dozen dips, this phrase popped into my head: *The darker the dot, the deeper the dip.*

It was a crazy slogan. It kept going through my head like a Coca-Cola jingle. Then I heard myself say it: "The darker the dot, the deeper the dip." What did it mean? I was puzzled, yet the phrase wouldn't stop. It was like the time on another trip when the song "Shuffle Off to Buffalo" played nonstop in my head all the way from Washington, D.C., to California. It was crazy.

In this case, though, it didn't take me long to figure out my new slogan: A big oil spot means a deep dip, a small oil spot means small dip. Simple, really.

Walking alongside a busy highway is a reminder of how fast we travel. There is no peace in such a walk. The roadside is a lonely wasteland and minor-league junkyard. There is nothing of interest in tourist terms, yet it is a worthwhile place to explore if you need to stretch.

I have just returned from a short walk alongside U.S. 395 south of Bishop. I had been cruising along at fifty-five when a sign caught my interest. By the time I could stop to take a photo, I was two hundred yards down the highway. So, with my camera, I hiked back as cars, trucks, and motor homes whizzed past in a hurry to be somewhere else.

Cows were grazing in a nearby pasture, and shadows half-covered the barren mountains to the east. Distant power poles looked like huge monsters. But the world at my feet was the most interesting. There were some native things, like weeds, but mostly it was unnatural stuff once hurled from a motor vehicle—food wrappers, broken glass, rusted bottle caps, and (of course) beer cans.

But nature was here, too, in the form of a hundred anthills. Each society did its business unaware of the passing steel monsters yards away. These worlds were marked by thousands of tiny sand pebbles formed into mounds resembling miniature cinder cones. I could have kicked away a world or two for fun, but what a terrible thing to do to the innocent creatures. It would be like a giant monster wiping out Boise with one evil swoop.

Anyway, I snapped my photo and was soon on my way. I didn't look again at the roadside. You can't see much from six feet up, going at fifty-five.

Everywhere you go in the West there are ants—big ants, tiny ants, ants that bite, ants that don't bite. You rest for a while at a picnic table and the next thing you know an ant is crawling up your leg.

Even at home there are ants. At my house they invade my kitchen every winter to escape the rain puddles outside. When you're talking about the number of ants in the West, you're talking trillions and trillions.

Ants do not generally interest me much except when they are in an Uncle Milton Ant Farm. Then, it is not the ants that are interesting, but the tunnels they build. I once owned an Uncle Milton Ant Farm. Every day the ants inside the ant farm would dig their tunnels a little farther. They'd haul the displaced sand to a spot in the top section of the ant farm, then return to tunnel some more.

For a few weeks it was pretty exciting watching these little fellows work. Then one day they hit plastic—the outer limits of their tabletop world. Being workaholics, they decided to dig more tunnels in the only place not already tunneled—the pile of sand from the original tunnels. But it wasn't long and that pile was tunneled out.

It was at this time that terminal depression took over. If you're an ant and there's no place left to dig, there's no reason to go on living, except to produce baby ants. But Uncle Milton doesn't provide queen ants, so each ant farm is ultimately terminal. So, bored to death and "mission accomplished," my ants died. All together, the society lasted a few months.

Ants are too small to play with, so they can never make adequate pets. And it's lucky for them they are so small, for an ant is a terrifyingly ugly creature if magnified even twenty or thirty times. Magnify one a thousand times and you have a scary movie monster.

Their little colonies are self-contained societies, and that is interesting to think about. Each colony's queen is its leader, just as in a few human colonies. Each colony has thousands of workers who do the work. They are like human workers except they don't get sick-leave or retirement benefits.

Among those workers are the scouts. These are the lone explorers that show up all alone in your kitchen or bathroom. It's their job to check out the scene, then report back. They are looking for food—which could be a few crumbs or an open box of Fruit Loops. They also search for dog food and cat food dishes, and ripe garbage cans.

Each year, I kill several hundred scouts. If I get them before they report back to Ant Central, then I keep their brothers and sisters from moving into my cupboard.

When I'm traveling, the scouts can spend many days exploring my house, and therefore have plenty of time to crawl home with news of my crumb-laden shelves. Needless to say, I have come home from a few trips to a houseful of ants. At such time, the mass-murderer in me surfaces. I gas 'em with Raid.

Mount Shasta is California's most beautiful mountain. On a clear day in the northern part of the state you can see it from at least a hundred miles away. People who live near it have remarkable stories about the 14,162-foot Cascade volcano.

The most remarkable stories are the legends about the mysterious people who supposedly live deep inside the mountain in apartments plated with gold. They are said to be descendants of an ancient society from Lemuria, a lost continent that sunk eons ago. In this secret colony, they preserve their ancient customs.

Lemurians are commonly described as graceful and tall— seven feet and up—with long, flowing hair, and slender necks adorned with beautiful decorative collars made of beads or precious stones. They dress in white robes and sandals.

Perhaps their most unusual physical characteristic is a walnut-size organ that protrudes from the center of their foreheads. This odd feature enables Lemurians to communicate among themselves by extrasensory perception.

Through the years, a few people have reported meeting Lemurians. One man said he visited them inside the mountain in a cavern two miles high, twenty miles long, and fifteen miles wide. A glowing mass of light provided the light of a summer day.

Another man reported that he fell asleep on Mount Shasta, to be awakened by a Lemurian who led him inside the mountain to his "cave, which was paved with gold." The Lemurian told the man that there were a series of tunnels left by volcanoes that were under the earth like freeways—a world within a world.

Lemurians supposedly mastered atomic energy, extrasensory perception, electronics, and science as long as eighteen thousand years ago. Back then, they knew how to propel boats using energy radiated from rocks. They had airships and flew them to Atlantis and other places. Today, people report seeing strange lights on the mountain. One explanation is that they are spacecraft coming and going from a fortress deep in the mountain.

Lemurians, it is said, possess supernatural powers that enable them to disappear at will—one reason why they aren't spotted very often. Their power also allows them to "will" an intruder away.

You can't visit the Mount Shasta area without reading or hearing about Lemurians. The local chamber of commerce must like the publicity because it attracts tourists. Still, talk to the local residents and you'll hear the popular disbelief about the Lemurians.

"I think there could have been a city of Lemuria, but as far as them being in the mountain, I don't believe it," said Jan Taylor, owner of Jan's Shear Magic Salon in Mount Shasta City, and a local resident for twenty-seven years.

"I don't believe any of it," said resident Pam Minafo. "I believe in things I can see."

Doug Gilliam of Doug's Barber Shop agreed. "I've been here thirty-four years and I've never seen any Lemurians. Hey, they can say anything, but let them produce it. They even said there's a black panther up there."

My guess is what's really inside Mount Shasta is dirt, rocks, and some lava.

I passed by some children playing in a field today and it reminded me of a time from my childhood. I was five, and lived in a neighborhood where there were five other little boys my age. Every day we built forts in vacant lots and played hide-and-seek in our backyards. But on one particular day we decided to do something different. Don't ask me why, but we decided to take off our

clothes and sit in a walnut tree. The tree had no leaves, but that
didn't matter to five little boys with five little minds set on perch-
ing bare-ass-naked in a tree that was begging to be perched upon.

So there we sat, pink and happy, watching the world pass by
as we discussed girls we didn't like, our kindergarten teacher, and
our respective inventories of marbles. A few yards away, motorists
drove by on their way to Fred's Market. Surely some of them must
have spotted us.

That was the only time we ever sat in that tree, and the only
time we ever took off our clothes together. Thinking back now, I
laugh at how odd we must have looked to those who saw us.

Today was a wonderful day in the rolling hills of northern
California. I spent the morning writing at my lakeside campsite at
Clear Lake State Park.

At noon, I packed up and headed to Kelseyville, where I
stopped to check out the bookstore. A young and attractive woman
named Lisa Knowles was working there, her first day on the job. I
was tempted to invite her to pack her bags right on the spot and
come along with me, but I didn't bother asking. I wasn't in the
mood for rejection. But I ended up staying an hour or so, and we
talked about writing, books, and life in Kelseyville. A blind cat was
bumping into walls, so I watched it with some curiosity while Lisa
waited on customers. After saying good-bye to Lisa and the blind
cat, I was back on the road heading north. I followed Route 20 past
beautiful Blue Lake. A few miles later I came to the sign POTTER
VALLEY. That sounded interesting, so I made a fast right and
headed down a curvy road. A Lakeport radio station was playing
good music—"Send In the Clowns" sung by Judy Collins, "I Can't
Stop Loving You" by Ray Charles, and other songs mostly from the
fifties and sixties.

I had no idea where the road led, or how I would get back to
the highway, but the scenery was so beautiful I didn't care. It was
a day to be lost—"Lost in America," like the title of the movie. It
was partly cloudy, and some of the clouds were hugging the tops of
the hills. I twisted and turned my way down the road—Mendocino
County Route 240—passing by red barns, old farmhouses, cows,
goats, horses, and sheep—and pretty fences of all types. Many of
the houses had fires going in their fireplaces, probably more for

ambience than warmth. I peeked inside some front windows, spotting a few people. Who were they? I wondered.

Then I pulled into Potter Valley and, honestly, I wouldn't have been surprised to see Jimmy Stewart and Donna Reed walking up the street as they did in the movie *It's a Wonderful Life*. Beaver and Wally Cleaver could have been playing catch in front of one of those Potter Valley houses.

The words *time warp* kept going around in my head, as if I had somehow slipped back a few decades. Kids were getting out of elementary school and the little girls were holding each other's hands on their way home.

I stopped at the Potter Valley Store, across from the post office, and bought a Snickers bar and a newspaper. I stayed ten minutes, observing Potter Valley folks going about their business. They greeted each other with smiles and by name, asking about jobs and family. As I walked back to the motor home, I noticed the postmaster staring outside at the passing traffic. I waved and he smiled and waved back.

After that I headed toward Lake Pillsbury, passing by a Louisiana Pacific lumber mill before arriving at an old one-lane bridge over the Eel River. I stopped for a minute, because it looked like it was about to collapse. I'm not usually afraid of bridges, but this one was decrepit, and there was a new bridge being built right next to it, which made me wonder what was wrong with the old one. But I went over it anyway and survived, and headed up the road, which turned fast to mud. I continued up for a couple of miles, having a hard time keeping my eyes off the beautiful river. But it was only an hour until dark and Lake Pillsbury—still twelve miles away—could have been closed up for all I knew. So I turned around.

I passed again through Potter Valley, then finally over to U.S. 101, which I followed north to Willits, where I had dinner at Mom's Place Restaurant. By the way, if you're interested in dentistry, then this is a good place to eat. If you choose the counter seat at the far right of the front door, there's a direct view into a nearby dentist's office. With some luck, you might see someone getting drilled.

After leaving Mom's, I found a campground a few miles outside town and settled in for the night.

*   *   *

George Washington would roll over in his grave if he knew how his name is being used to sell cars, clocks, underwear, and about everything else. It's Washington's birthday today and everybody is running George Washington Birthday Specials. The radio station in Lakeport is running an ad for some business (I can't remember the name) that says "George Washington was born on two twenty-two, so in celebration we'll give the first two hundred and twenty-two customers who stop by a cherry pie for only two dollars and twenty-two cents."

What an honor! Selling cheap pies in the name of our founding father. If Washington were alive, he'd be talking with his lawyer.

I stopped by for coffee this morning at Bee's Cafe in Clearlake Oaks because of the statue of a gorilla in a chef's outfit out front. Beth Bowman owns the coffee shop; Bee is deceased. The gorilla is mechanical, but broken. He used to be a chef that waved to passing motorists. Then he broke two years ago. Last Halloween, Beth's husband Ron put a gorilla mask on the mechanical chef and people thought it was funny. So the mask stayed.

All I ordered was coffee, and it was fine. Another customer complimented my waitress, Wendy, on the buckwheat pancakes, so I assume they were good.

Bee's Cafe is also a gift shop, mostly selling hanging plants and brass things. I liked the brass-elephant telephone, which at eighty-five dollars seemed like a good deal. I also liked a sign on the wall: RULE NO.1: THE BOSS IS ALWAYS RIGHT. RULE NO.2: IF THE BOSS IS WRONG, SEE RULE NO.1.

I can't say for sure if the food is good at Bee's, but the humor is.

I just finished reading *The Redwood Record* newspaper, which I bought at a newsstand yesterday. Unfortunately, much of what I bought wasn't newspaper at all, but inserts for supermarkets. I weighed everything on my postal scale. The newspaper weighed three ounces, the inserts five ounces. So out of my 25-cent investment I paid 9.37 cents for news and 15.62 cents for ad inserts. I wish they would have left out the inserts and charged me a dime.

Fast food in Grass Valley isn't a hamburger or hot dog. It's a pasty (pass-tee), a Cornish meat pie with a local history nearly as old as the California mother-lode town itself. Visiting Grass Valley without eating a pasty is like visiting the Napa Valley without tasting wine.

The pasty arrived here in the 1860s with immigrants from Cornwall, England, who came to work in the gold mines. It was a very popular dish back home in Cornwall—sort of the "Big Mac" of its day.

"The old saying was that the devil himself wouldn't go to Cornwall because they'd put him in a pasty," said Irene Clemence, part-owner of Grass Valley's King Richard's Pasties.

The Cornish had mined tin in southern England for centuries, so were experienced hard-rock miners. Before long, thousands had emigrated to America to work in the mines. Many of these "Cousin Jacks" came to Grass Valley. In the mines, pasties were popular at lunchtime. The compact meal was tasty, filling, and nourishing. A miner would use the flame of a candle to heat his pasty in a special lunch pail.

Today, three local businesses turn out more than a million of the small, oval-shaped meat pies a year, many for the descendants of the original Cousin Jacks. Restaurants all over town have them on their menus.

If you are in Grass Valley, be sure to try one.

It's possible there could be a traffic jam in Tennant. If everybody in town decided to drive somewhere at the same time they might clog up the main street for a minute or so.

Tennant doesn't seem to belong in California—it's so small, so remote. A paved Siskiyou County road off U.S. Highway 97 turns to dirt a few miles from town, then turns back to pavement, but only through town.

Some town. About eighty folks live in Tennant, down from eight hundred when it was a company town for International Paper Company's Long-Bell division. Back then there was a hotel, grocery store, barber shop, school, railroad station, library, post office—about anything the loggers could want. Today, there are ninety-nine houses (not all occupied), a community center, and the Tennant Store and Cafe and its adjoining Long-Bell Saloon.

Long-Bell shut down in 1957 and donated the town to the Veterans of Foreign Wars, which figured it could use it to house some of its pensioned veterans. But that didn't work out, so the VFW sold Tennant to Clarence Bullock, who fixed things up and started selling the two-bedroom company houses for thirty-five hundred dollars. Today, those same houses go for about eighteen thousand to thirty thousand dollars.

The Tennant Store carries a few grocery items, but not many. Most residents drive to Klamath Falls, Oregon, for supplies—about a half-day round-trip. If you want a daily newspaper you get it by mail—a day late.

The busiest time of year is hunting season. "We make most of our money those weekends," said Tennant Store and Cafe owner Theresa Kiss, who hauls in her own supplies because it isn't worth anybody else's while to bring them in. Another big time is in September, when Tennant residents stage an annual barbecue. But most of the time visitors only trickle in, sometimes intentionally, sometimes because they're lost. Said Kiss: "If a strange car comes into town, people ask each other who it is."

It occurred to me today that a small town is a place where you cannot be cited for running a red light. The reason would be that there are no red lights—or green ones, either.

If you have traveled Highway 101 through the California redwood country, you have no doubt seen the Tree House. It's a giant, living coastal redwood tree, the inside of which is billed as the "tallest one-room house in the world." It's right alongside the road, so it's hard to miss.

Howard and Annette Wilson have owned the Tree House and its gift shop for fourteen years. It was opened in the late 1920s by a woman named Lilley, who sold soda pop and postcards from the tree's belly—a 560-square-foot room with charred walls and a cone-shaped ceiling 50 feet high. The tree was burned badly three hundred years ago, which accounts for the blackened walls.

The tree's statistics:

- Age: 4,000 years.
- Circumference: 101.5 feet
- Diameter: 33 feet
- Height: 250 feet (and still growing)

The highway out front wasn't much in the twenties when Mrs. Lilley opened the Tree House. It was built with convict labor; the workers slept in the tree.

For more than sixty years now, people have been stopping by the Tree House to gawk and buy souvenirs; third and even fourth generations of original visitors now come from all parts of the world.

Old-timers have tales to tell. "A woman in her nineties came in one day and she had a big smile on her face," Howard Wilson recalled. "She said she once slept in the tree. She and her husband were driving through the redwoods, and they decided to spend the night here; they even built a fire. The next morning, she said, they were awakened by the sound of a mountain lion on the hill. She turned to her husband and said, 'It's time to go.' "

The Wilsons are the third owners. Howard was at the counter when I visited—selling postcards, miniature redwood trees, and all kinds of Tree House things—key rings, pocket knives, T-shirts— you name it.

He explained some interesting things about the Tree House:

• The floor from the tree to the back of the gift shop: "It raises up about eight to ten inches from the front to the back. It used to be level. The tree is still growing, so the roots are raising it. The window inside the tree cracked once from the growth."

• The cobwebs inside the tree: "We never touch them. If we cleaned them out, the spiders would just put them back. We clean the windows, but the cobwebs come right back."

• The lone light bulb at the very inside top of the cone-shaped ceiling, fifty feet up: "It's been going for at least thirty years. I'm not sure if it's dim because of low wattage or because it's just so dirty."

• The photo of the cat on the wall. "That's Wheaters. He was here from 1968 to 1986 when he died. I bet a million people petted that cat. Three years after he died, people still ask for him. He was a fixture."

Wilson said men seem more interested in the tree than women. "The women see the gift shop and they head right in— that's their nature. The men will stay in the tree for ten minutes checking it out. They're impressed with the size. People are im-

47

pressed with redwoods. They see pictures on postcards, and they think they just look like trees. Then they come here and they say, 'Hey, I didn't know they were that big!' I could have sold this tree for a lot of money. A guy from Florida said it was the best thing he had ever seen in his life. He told me he'd buy it if I could get it to Florida alive."

Wilson said the log cabin motel rooms out back are no longer for rent. Clark Gable and Carole Lombard stayed there, the story goes.

What's so special about a four-leaf clover except it's supposed to bring you good luck? Who says?

I came upon some clover today in the redwoods and decided to search for one with four leaves. I searched for about two minutes, then stopped, thinking: *What's so special about a four-leaf clover? It's only a piece of grass, a mutant, no less. A two-headed calf is also a mutant. Does it bring luck?*

So instead of spending an hour finding a four-leaf clover, I spent two seconds finding a three-leafed one. I think it's great. I put it on my dash to bring me luck. So far, so good.

I was just sitting outside looking at the stars and listening to a Gordon Lightfoot tape on my Walkman stereo. I'm camped in Richardson's Grove State Park, in a magnificent grove of coastal redwoods.

This is the first night in a long time that the sky has been cloudfree and the air warm enough to be outside at night. So I marveled at a star-filled sky. Tonight it was especially beautiful because the stars were framed by a half dozen redwoods. The view through those redwoods was like a window to the universe.

I was thinking how special it is to gaze upon other worlds. On Earth, we're lucky to see twenty or thirty miles at any one time. But in the night sky we can view sights so far away that in a lifetime of space travel we could reach but a few.

If you or I had lived indoors all our life, and then one day we were permitted outside to witness such a night sky, we would be awed. It would be better than the Oregon coast, Yosemite, or an Arizona sunset. We should never take a skyful of stars for granted.

I'm glad I don't know much about the sky. If I studied astronomy, then I would probably spend a lot of time looking for certain stars and galaxies. I'd be so caught up in technicalities, I wouldn't be able to do any pondering.

As it is, when dark approaches, I sit in my lawn chair and scan the sky for the first star. Once sighted, I make a wish, and then count each additional star up to about twenty. Then I sit back and let my mind wander. Muscles relax, problems disappear, and I'm happy. I don't know exactly what I'm seeing—only that it's huge, far away, and beautiful.

I don't want to learn anything technical about what I'm seeing up there. The saying "ignorance is bliss" is true in this case.

The flashlight is a great invention. When you live in a city, you don't have much use for one, except maybe when you fix your plumbing or explore your basement. But in the woods, you use a flashlight a lot.

When you think about it, a flashlight is an amazing tool. You flip a switch and a beam of light zooms out from a cylinder you hold effortlessly in your hand. Imagine what a caveman or cavewoman would have thought of such a device.

Just a few minutes ago, I was fumbling for a can of soda pop at my picnic table. It was pitch black outside, so I couldn't locate the can. But no problem: I just reached into my pocket for my little flashlight, turned it on, pointed the beam of light, and found what I was searching for. A flashlight isn't just a handy device, it's a small miracle.

CHAPTER TWO

ARIZONA

Dʀɪᴠɪɴɢ a two-lane across the Arizona desert today, I looked to the sky and saw the contrail of a westbound 747. How high was the plane? Maybe forty thousand feet?

Around me were only sagebrush and a weathered billboard for a distant Dairy Queen. But up there, more than seven miles away, a silver cylinder of civilization sped toward California. Aboard were people, suitcases, restrooms—and even a service elevator to go from one deck to the other. And the whole thing was heading west as fast as a speeding bullet.

I wondered what was going on inside. A stewardess serving a martini to a businessman? A UCLA student reading her economics lesson? A little boy making his third trip to the bathroom? Maybe a talkative fat guy with bad breath was offending the young woman in the next seat. Perhaps *Back to the Future* was playing on a movie screen. Was a steward or stewardess aboard the elevator at that very moment? It didn't seem right that up there in the sky someone was riding an elevator while I was on the ground below dodging jackrabbits and Gila monsters.

I watched the plane for a few minutes, then it disappeared from my sight; in an hour, I figured, it would be landing in Los Angeles. Me, I'd be a few miles up the road, sipping a Coke, smelling the sagebrush, and maybe even singing "I'm Just an Okie from Muskogee" with Merle Haggard, if it came on the radio.

The West looks different from forty thousand feet all right—especially at night when the earth below appears to be a huge black sea with tiny islands of light. You can guess the cities, but you seldom know if you're right. Grand Junction, Casper, and even Las Vegas seem so small from forty thousand feet. The outposts—Ely, Nevada; Winslow, Arizona; Thermopolis, Wyoming; Baker, California—are even harder to identify. At night, a town of a thousand looks like a pinhead from seven miles up.

Finding highways is like playing a connect-the-numbers game, except you connect headlights—the tiniest pinpoints of light in the vast blackness. Draw an imaginary line between the lights and you've got the road.

When you fly coast to coast, with nothing much to do, you can look outside your window and marvel at the unpopulated West. You can marvel that in a world of gridlocked freeways, smoggy air, and cellular telephones, there are still places with one-room schools, general stores, and people who believe any town with a stoplight is too damn big.

John Weber had a midlife crisis and ended up in the rattle-snake business in the Arizona ghost town of Gleeson. He and his wife Sandra live in a modest green trailer house, and for a few months each year they hunt the poisonous reptiles in the surrounding hills.

For every nine hours they hunt, they get one. Later, they use its skin to decorate a belt, bracelet, earrings, or even a necktie. They call their business Rattlesnake Crafts. Headquarters is an old thirty-foot trailer that was their house until last year.

It's the only business in Gleeson. The tavern closed up a few

John and Sandy Weber, Gleeson, Arizona

years back. The best attraction besides the Webers' place is a burro named Claudette that roams the dirt streets looking for food.

The Webers came from Chicago nine years ago in search of a new life. He was a contract administrator for an aviation company, she a secretary. "Here we were, forty-five, trying to decide what to do with the rest of our lives," said John. So they quit their jobs not knowing what lay ahead. Their coworkers didn't understand. "How can you quit and know what to do?" they asked John.

They came west with only what they could fit into the car, settled into a rented house near Phoenix and began searching for rattlesnakes. They barely existed at first. But they started catching rattlesnakes and turning them into different things, and business gradually picked up. After a few years, they moved to Gleeson—a dusty ghost town with hundreds of rattlesnakes and jackrabbits for every human being.

Today they are happy, although not materially rich. They almost apologize for owning a microwave oven, VCR, and color television. Until this year, Sandra washed clothes in a bucket with a squeeze-ringer. They live on the amount of money some people make in car payments. "There aren't any Joneses out here to compete with," said Sandra.

They drive a weathered Toyota pickup with 272,000 miles on its original engine. Once a week they go to town, usually Sierra Vista. They would never move back to Chicago or any other big town. Their old friends and coworkers stop by now asking for retirement tips.

John has evolved from a city man to a country man. "It took him a long time to give up his money belt," said Sandra. "I told him cowboys don't wear money belts."

Although the handful of Gleeson residents are a close-knit group, they come together mostly only in time of need. The rest of the time, the Webers' friends are the tourists who stop by and the coyotes that howl in the night. Of course, there's Claudette the burro, but her turf is the entire town.

At home, once in a while I'll make a wrong turn and end up in an unexpected part of town. It's no big deal. Yesterday, though, I made a wrong turn near Tucson and ended up in Phoenix instead of in the state of New Mexico as I had planned.

I was traveling at night, playing my radio, enjoying the warm night air. I wasn't paying much attention to where I was going. I guess I must have turned right when I should have turned left, because a couple of hours later I saw a road sign: PHOENIX, 53 miles. Well, I figured I could see New Mexico later, so I just continued on, and spent a couple of days around Phoenix before heading up to Globe and Payson.

I don't really have a point here. I was just thinking how funny it is that you can make a wrong turn in Tucson and end up in Phoenix instead of New Mexico.

It was a beautiful evening, so I decided to sit outside and visit my friend the night sky.

Tonight there was no moon, only a black sky lit by a million stars. Across the middle was the Milky Way, a welcome friend I hadn't seen for a while. Tonight's star-gazing was better because of a cassette tape my father had made for me of some of his favorite country songs. There was a time when I didn't care for country music, but as I get older my tastes change.

The stars were framed by three Douglas firs near my campsite and the silhouette of pine trees on a distant ridge. One shooting star after another streaked across the sky, each marking its final moment of an eternal spaceflight. I made a few wishes, even though I knew only the first one counted.

All the while, I listened to one beautiful song after another. And as I immersed myself in the music and the expanse above, I thought how wonderful it is to be alive.

When you study the nighttime sky and its million stars, you may feel humbled. Seeing stars and other worlds so far away makes our Earth seem small and most of our problems inconsequential.

Our planet is but a pinpoint in the universe. If you can stare at the nighttime sky and still fret that you can't afford a Rolex watch or a new BMW or a second home at the beach, then you have not seen the message of the night sky. It tells us that life is short, that life is precious, that life is beautiful, and that to worry about petty things—acquiring material possessions, for example—is not important.

The sky can teach these things and more, but only to those who want to know.

I noticed something else about the night sky. In the country, you can see stars all the way down to the horizon. In the city, the lights drown them out.

My campsite in the Coconino National Forest is surrounded by trees, but a meadow is only a short walk away. I walked into it at about ten o'clock and was greeted by a magnificent sky. When I looked straight up, all I could see was sky—from one edge of my vision to another. I thought that this is what outer space must look like if you were passing through it in a spaceship—a black expanse with a million pinpoints of light. Nothing else. It was an inspiring sight.

I write a lot about the nighttime sky, maybe too much. I never realized until recently how much it means to me. I had always taken it for granted. Now, in the country so much, the sky and its stars have become good friends. Spending time looking above not only calms and inspires me, but puts the everyday problems of my life in perspective. I call it sky therapy. You might want to try it.

*   *   *

Today I drove about two hundred miles of Interstate 40 from Albuquerque, New Mexico, to Holbrook, Arizona. Per square mile, there are more Indian trading posts here than anywhere else in America. I'm pretty sure of it.

I visited Indian City, Chief Yellowhorse, Fort Courage, Indian Ruins, and Indian Village, but I passed many more. One advertised the world's largest teepee (six stories). Another advertised live buffalo. One invited me to walk through an "Authentic Navajo Hogan," a native house.

I stopped at Indian Village to see the "Navajo weaving a rug." The only Navajo was a woman eating a cheeseburger. So I watched her. An older couple was buying gifts for their grandchildren. "Well, we bought *her* something Indian, so we have to buy *him* something Indian," the woman told her husband.

There are so many billboards along the highway advertising these places that you hardly see any countryside. I'll bet there are twenty-five billboards per mile along some stretches.

While these souvenir shops sell legitimate Indian-made goods, much of the merchandise is junk. Half the gross national product of

Billboard on I-40, Arizona

Taiwan is here. Hong Kong and Mexico are also well represented.

My favorite stop was Indian Village, which is right on top of the Continental Divide. I liked using the bathroom; it was the first one I ever used on the Continental Divide. After flushing the toilet, a question popped into my mind, but I didn't have the foggiest idea of the answer. So I stood there, thinking. As the water flushed away, I kept thinking and thinking. Drying my hands, I was still thinking. Now, half a day later, I'm still thinking. Of course, I was wondering which ocean that particular flush would end up in.

I don't mean to offend you, but I have a complaint I can no longer ignore. What I'm talking about is the awful toilet paper in public restrooms. It could do double duty as wax paper. This paper is so slick it repels water. Put a roll in the rain for a while then examine it; it will be dry. Throw a roll in a lake and it will still be afloat in an hour.

The worst paper is in Forest Service outhouses. It comes in little six-inch squares. Blow your nose with a piece of this and you will miss. Somewhere in America salesmen roam around selling this paper to campgrounds and service stations. How do they sleep at night?

We're only a few years away from the twenty-first century, yet we still have those old-fashioned sinks with two water spigots, one for hot water, one for cold. They make no sense. You have two choices when you use this type of sink: freeze your hands in cold water or burn them in hot water. If you want to wash with warm water, you turn on both spigots and move your hands from one to another—at a Superman-kind of speed. What you are actually doing is burning your hands, then cooling them so fast you can't feel the burn. What you get is "psychologically warm" water.

Sure, you can fill up the sink and wash that way. The disadvantage of this method, of course, is the minute you start washing, the water gets dirty. This sink should be illegal.

I just did something in a public restroom to stay healthy: I dried my hands with one of those blow-dry machines. You push a button and warm air comes shooting out. You rub your hands under there for twenty seconds or so, and theoretically they get dried. By using the machine you "prevent the hazards of disease." That's what's printed right on the machine. I guess paper towels can spread disease. I don't understand how you can catch something from a paper towel, but if the blow-dry machine says so, then I'm all for using hot air.

The only thing I wonder is if I might pick up some germs after using the machine. That's when I rub my hands on the back of my Levi's.

One souvenir item I nearly bought earlier at Indian Village was a $1.69 jackalope (jack-a-lope) piggy bank. A jackalope is a mythical jackrabbit with horns. Most souvenir shops in the rural West sell jackalopes or at least jackalope postcards. These particular jackalopes were about six inches tall. It didn't say where they were made, but I suspect Taiwan or Hong Kong. They couldn't have been made in America for the price.

You can figure that Indian Village makes a 50 to 100 percent profit, which means it pays from about eighty-five cents to a dollar ten for each jackalope. The store buys the jackalopes from a wholesaler, who buys the jackalopes from an importer, who buys the jackalopes from the company that made them in the first place. So three companies make a profit before the jackalopes even arrive at Indian Village.

Somewhere along the line, one of those companies has to pay to ship the jackalopes halfway around the world. Some sea captain, coming into port, has to fill out a slip announcing his cargo: "Jackalopes," he writes.

My guess is that whoever makes those jackalopes gets ten cents apiece for their work. No company in America can make a jackalope for a dime.

Today I asked the clerk at the Texaco station for a cash receipt. I always ask for a receipt, as my gasoline expense is tax deductible. But do you know what the clerk said? She said, "Okeydokey."

Okeydokey? What an odd word! Yet many of us use it. Why? Where did it come from?

WOODEN INDIANS. WE SHIP. That's what the sign said outside the Hassayampa River Trading Company, which is along Highway

60 near Morristown. Being a curious fellow, I decided to stop and learn how you ship a wooden Indian.

I counted seventeen wooden Indians out front of the trading post, plus some cattle skulls, a sign that said AUTHENTIC INDIAN JEWELRY, and another sign that said AMERICAN EXPRESS ACCEPTED HERE.

Inside, a guy about fifty-five was wearing a cowboy hat and slacks, and he was looking at me coldly like maybe I was from the IRS. He was checking out my notepad and my camera, and he looked like he had a chip on his shoulder.

Now, he wasn't mean-looking in a physical way—it was just his unfriendly demeanor. Physically, he looked more like a dentist than a trader of Indian goods.

"I see you sell wooden Indians," I said with a friendly grin.

"Yup," he answered with no grin at all.

"You ship 'em, too. I see that by your sign."

"Yup."

I figured maybe he was shy, and that was why he didn't talk much. So I decided to walk around and let him see I was up to no harm. I found some three-dollar Indian dolls from Hong Kong, some domestic bullhorns, a rack of postcards, and Arizona T-shirts in various shapes and colors. But mostly there was a lot of good Indian jewelry, and some good leather gun holsters and wallets, and lots of rocks, and a wall stacked with boxes of moccasins. It was a better Indian shop than those along the Interstates.

The guy, meanwhile, was watching me like I was going to pocket a tomahawk, or make off with this long broomstick with a skull on its end.

"What kind of skull is that?"

"Coyote."

"Does it signify something?"

"Maybe to the Indians, not to me."

He was not opening up to me at all. It was time to try kindness.

"You sure do have a lot of good things in here," I said, smiling. I waited for him to open up—to say: "Why thank you, I'm real proud of all the fine Indian crafts I've got here."

But he didn't say that. He just said: "Yup."

So kindness didn't work.

"Have many Germans come in here lately?" (I asked that

question because I had seen so many Germans on my own trip.)

"Germans, French, and English," he answered.

"Did you sell any wooden Indians to the Germans?"

"Nope."

I was losing hope that he'd tell me about the wooden Indian shipping business. And I really wanted to know!

He just stood by his card table staring at me. And even though he wasn't talking, I knew what he was thinking. *Who the heck are you, you dumb city-slicker, and why are you asking all these questions?*

So I changed the subject. "I see you have a Navajo hogan outside. Do the Navajo live around here?"

"They live in Arizona."

"But do many live around *here?*"

"A few."

"I haven't seen any other hogans around here."

"We built this one."

"What about the wooden Indians? Do you make them yourself?"

"Nope, I buy 'em locally."

"Oh, somebody around here makes 'em? In Wickenburg?"

"No, locally."

I waited for more words. Nothing . . .

Well, this conversation was going nowhere, and this fellow wasn't solving my curiosity one bit about how you ship a wooden Indian. I wanted to know things like: Do you ship a wooden Indian by UPS? If so, does UPS pick up? How much does it cost to ship a wooden Indian? And who wraps up a wooden Indian so it can be shipped?

And, most of all, I wanted to know who buys a wooden Indian. That's what I wanted to know. That's what I didn't find out. Sorry.

Jeepers! For about twenty miles along I-10 in southeastern Arizona, there are a bunch of billboards advertising THE THING? You feel you should stop even though you know it's probably just another tourist trap with three-dollar Indian dolls from Taiwan and Indian headbands from South Carolina. Still, I stopped.

What I found was two-thirds souvenir shop and one-third Dairy Queen. Inside, there were postcards and belts and toy tomahawks and a thousand other items. I checked out the $6.99 bull-horns from Mexico but decided they wouldn't look good on my motor home's grill, so I didn't buy one.

Then I saw it—the mysterious cavelike entrance to the back where you can see the actual "Thing." Admission is seventy-five cents, which seemed like a good deal to see something mysterious. Right up next to the entrance is a big color TV, with people talking about "The Thing." "What is The Thing?" an announcer asks, and people say, "I don't know but it's really neat and mysterious." And all these people are smiling and looking like they got their seventy-five-cents' worth. So I paid my three quarters and went inside.

Boy, it was a big disappointment at first, because the cave leads to the backyard of the souvenir shop. But a concrete pathway with big yellow footprints leads to "The Thing," so it would be premature at this point to figure you've been ripped off.

There are four buildings, and the first three are really crummy and not worth even twenty-five cents. There are cars and old wagons and tractors and pieces of driftwood painted up with faces, and a bunch of other stuff that would be in the storerooms of most museums.

Take the tractor, for example. Its sign says, EARLY-MADE TRACTOR WAS REALLY THE "THING" FOR REPLACING FOUR-LEGGED HORSE POWER. Or how about the 1849 covered wagon? WAGONS LIKE THIS . . . TRANSPORTED OUR FOREFATHERS. CURRENT MODELS ARE CALLED CAMPERS. The 1932 Buick sign says, THIS ANTIQUE CAR WAS REALLY THE "THING" FOR TRANSPORTATION IN 1932.

There's even a 1937 Rolls-Royce that MAY HAVE BEEN USED BY ADOLF HITLER. Those words MAY HAVE BEEN made me very suspicious about this exhibit. And there was a lot more mediocre stuff. By the entrance to the fourth building I was feeling like the real "Thing" here was ripping off tourists.

Then, I entered Building Four. And there, right before my eyes, was the very thing I had paid seventy-five cents to see: "The Thing." For the next ten minutes I checked it out, and I'm here to report it is worth between fifty and seventy-five cents all by itself.

"The Thing" is a mummy—whether man or woman isn't clear because there's a hat covering the part of the body that might provide such information. But "The Thing" lies in a glass coffin, and it's got what looks like a baby (which looks phony) in its arms. You can look up close and see the ribs of "The Thing" and some bones in its legs. "The Thing" is weird and eerie and dusty and pretty interesting for an Interstate mummy.

People were coming by and staring at "The Thing," and some were claiming it was a ripoff—that "The Thing" was a fake—but some were impressed and wide-eyed. I took a vote, and two thirds of the people thought "The Thing" was artificial. But they weren't experts, so who knows?

Anyway, that's what you see for seventy-five cents at "The Thing!" It's a pretty good place to stop. And if you're hungry you can even grab a burger at the Dairy Queen.

Home to George and Javonna Carrell is about anywhere along the road, a life of Interstates and truck stops and greasy food and uncertainty. They drive an eighteen-wheeler truck, and in an average year cover 125,000 miles in most of the continental states. Most nights they share the twin bed in the truck's sleeper compartment. "You get tired of it, and taking showers in truck stops gets cold," said Javonna, "but you get to see a lot." They were heading west from El Paso, Texas, to Henderson, Nevada, when I met them at "The Thing?" tourist stop on I-10.

I asked George if it's true that truckers know the best places to eat. "No," he said. "Truckers eat where they can park. But if you see some tractors without their trailers in front of a place, then that's a good place to eat."

Kingman, Arizona, has 12,500 residents, which was a big surprise to me. I figured the population would be about half of that. The Steak Barn restaurant there offers rattlesnake as an appetizer. It tastes almost exactly like fried chicken except it is very salty. The main street in Kingman—the old Route 66—is Andy Devine Avenue, named for the western character actor. It received its new name in 1955 on the television program *This Is Your Life* when Andy appeared as a guest. Andy, by the way, was born in Flagstaff, but his family moved to Kingman when he was a year old, so that's where he grew up.

Andy Devine is Kingman's biggest claim to fame. It seems odd to me that a town would get so excited about a so-so actor. It's not like he was Clark Gable or John Wayne. But if that's all you've got to brag about, I guess you go with what you have.

In Fresno, California, the folks got so excited about a Los Angeles Dodger baseball player named Steve Garvey that they named a high school after him. A school in Yuma, Arizona, is named after Ronald Reagan.

I'd be honored if a school would name itself for me. I don't know why they would, but if any school wants to, it has my permission. I think Chuck Elementary School has a nice ring to it. What do you think?

I'm real excited just thinking about this.

The wind is howling here in Kingman. Out the back window of the motor home, a tumbleweed is racing past like it's late to work.

Yesterday I hit a huge piece of tumbleweed. I was speeding along at about fifty-five miles an hour, and the tumbleweed came out of nowhere toward me at about twenty-five. That adds up to an eighty-mile-per-hour crash.

Normally if a vehicle and something as large as that giant weed collide, there's serious damage. But in this case nothing happened but a little noise. The motor home just kept rolling as the tumbleweed splattered to bits. Ten seconds later the incident was pretty much forgotten.

If you've got to hit something, better to hit a tumbleweed than a cow.

I have grown to like tumbleweed. You hardly ever see tumbleweed in a big town—especially not places like New York City or Atlanta. I wonder if a tumbleweed ever blew across any street in Manhattan. Probably not.

Tumbleweed is my friend when I am roaming the West. I associate it with wide-open country populated by roadrunners, jackrabbits, lizards—and most important—souvenir shops with jackalopes. I also associate it with clean air and two-lane roads with practically no traffic.

So, to me, tumbleweed is pretty terrific.

I had a bad experience last night. I was camped in a free, out-of-the-way Forest Service campground near Superior. I had pulled in after dark, so I really didn't know what it looked like. It was almost empty, at least in the section where I camped.

As I lay in bed, I thought how quiet it was. There were some coyotes howling in the distance, but that was it. There was no traffic noise or other sound of civilization. I was falling asleep at about 11:30 P.M. when a loud voice awoke me. It was a man's, and he was in the next campsite, using the foulest language I'd heard in a long time. I thought I was dreaming. But then there was a second voice and he was also swearing loudly. Then, one of the men turned on his car stereo. Music blasted from speakers in the open doors. The volume was so high the sound was distorted.

I couldn't believe my ears—that anyone could be so rude. The music had drowned out their voices, but I guessed they were either drunk or on drugs. I couldn't imagine that a person in an unaltered state could be so insensitive.

I endured this for ten minutes. I figured I had three choices: stay put and hope they went away, which could mean hours of sleeplessness; walk outside and tell the creeps to shut up; or find another campground.

As I considered my options, the only other camper in the area got into his car, started it up, and prepared to leave. His headlights beamed on the two men—who were mean-looking dudes. Both were drinking beer.

I made my decision: I wasn't going to stay—and I wasn't about to tell these two Blutos to shut up. It would be two against one if they didn't like me, and those are crummy odds. So in five minutes I was on the road. I wanted to report the camp-busters. I searched for a police car in Superior, but found none because the town was sound asleep.

At 1:00 A.M. I pulled into Lost Dutchman State Park in Apache Junction and was soon in bed. When I awoke the next morning, I thought about the two guys: I hoped they had terrible hangovers.

Now I suppose that if I tell some people about this incident they will remind me that it is a dangerous society in which we live, and I'd better be careful.

I, of course, will tell them that I am not worried. I will say, as I have said so many times before, that I have camped in literally hundreds of campgrounds from California to Colorado and New Mexico to Montana, and in all those times I have not been murdered even once.

* * *

In the places where I dine, you seldom get a fabric tablecloth. Two nights ago, at Kovak's Korner in Apache Junction, I was served on cloth, even though my chicken dinner was only $3.50.

It got me thinking about tablecloths and silverware. Does it ever seem odd to you that when you dine out, the first thing you do is take the clean napkin from under the silverware to put on your lap, even though you have to place the silverware back on the exposed table? What about that table? It could be dirty.

I once saw a woman change her baby's diapers on a table at Taco Bell. Would you want your silverware on that spot if you were the next customer?

In the old days, tables were covered with clean *cloth* table-cloths. On top of the tablecloth was a clean cloth napkin, and on top of that was the silverware. When you removed the napkin for your lap, the silverware remained on a clean tablecloth. You knew your silverware wasn't sitting on germs. Today, you never know what it's sitting on.

I drove through Phoenix on surface streets from Apache Junction to Sun City. Now first of all, I say, "I drove on surface streets." For you readers in rural areas who've never seen a road that wasn't on the surface, "surface street" is a big-city word meaning any street but a freeway. The surface street I chose through Phoenix was a combination of U.S. Highways 60, 89, and Business 10.

It was a terrific drive, even though it took ninety minutes to go from one end of town to the other. Of course, I stopped a half dozen times to take photos. What I liked the most were the old motels. There must be a hundred of them along that stretch. I assume this was the main road before Phoenix got its freeways.

Here were some of the motels I spotted: Rose Bowl Motel, Log Cabin Motel, Near Town Motel, Old Faithful Inn Motel, Lazy-A Motel, Refrigerated Motel, Golden Goose Motel, Navajo Motel, Rock Haven Motel, Trails End Motel, and the Two Palms Motel. What good names! They don't name motels like that anymore. Today, except for cheap motels—motels are called inns, lodges, motor lodges, or even hotels. Only chains like Motel 6 are called motels.

Today, some of the rooms in those old Phoenix motels cost as little as ten dollars a night. I didn't go into any of the rooms, but I wouldn't expect elegance. I'd expect a little cracked paint and a saggy bed with some miles. Today, to attract guests, the new lodges advertise cable TV, microwave ovens, VCRs and hot tubs. Back in the old days, motels advertised TV (plain ol'), kitchenettes, and refrigeration (air conditioning). Those were big deals. In the fancy places, you might even get a Magic Fingers machine.

I love those Magic Fingers machines—I even hot-wired one once in North Carolina, which proves that even an honest man like me can be driven to a criminal act in the pursuit of pleasure.

After a long day's drive, there is nothing like relaxing on your rented bed, plopping a quarter into a Magic Fingers, and then savoring the soothing vibrations from one of the few items manufactured in America that lives up to its name.

I estimate that in my lifetime I have deposited at least thirty dollars in Magic Fingers machines—bringing me hours and hours of vibrasonic pleasure. What else costs so little and provides so much?

My last Magic Fingers experience was in 1987 in Bakersfield, California. I was amazed to see that the Magic Fingers still only cost a quarter—the same as twenty years before!

There in Bakersfield, I emptied my pockets of change, placed it on the nightstand by my pleasure machine, stripped down to my underwear, lay down on my double bed, and prepared to be vibrated into a heaven on Earth. I also turned on the color TV to watch *Eyewitness News* to make the experience even better.

It was terrific—Magic Fingers and *Eyewitness News*. What a combo! It doesn't come any better than that.

It's November and ads for cold remedies have started running on television. Do you know what that means? To me it means that in a few weeks I can expect to feel a sudden tingle in my throat followed by a sneeze and then a cough. And for the next seven days I will suffer.

Have you ever suspected that in about mid-October, the companies that make cold remedies release secret colonies of germs into the air?

I have.

We should all leave our earthly existence with something to show for our years. It was with this thought in mind that I pointed my motor home toward tiny Congress, Arizona. I only stayed fifteen minutes, but that was long enough. Now, when someone asks me what I have accomplished in my lifetime, I can answer with all honesty that I spent some time in Congress.

I awoke this morning to the smell of exhaust fumes. The guy in the motor home next to mine had started up his engine. This happens once in a while when you park your house somewhere other than in a campground.

One morning I awoke while dreaming about traffic. I don't remember the details, but I was probably stuck in traffic at 7:00 A.M. on the San Bernardino Freeway around Pomona or Upland. I'm sure I was tossing and turning and working up a sweat with images of gridlock in my head—horns honking, motorcyclists weaving in and out of lanes, and guys in gray suits drinking coffee out of AM/PM Mini-Mart mugs in one hand while talking on their cellular phones in the other hand. It was horrible.

Then I woke up. It turned out the source of my agony was a guy in a motor home starting up his engine. In the process, he was making noise and sending engine exhaust my way.

Waking up to a nightmare like that is no fun.

Yesterday, in the campground at Chiricahua National Monument, a fellow was washing out his backpacking pans in the men's room toilet. It was the strangest sight I'd seen since I saw a woman changing her baby's diapers on a table at a Taco Bell. I was glad he didn't invite me to join him for a meal.

My picnic table is all carved up. Quite a few of the carvings are expressions of love. There's TOM & PAM, VG & RF, MICH & MONY, and MICHAEL & DELY. Each expression is surrounded by the carved shape of a heart.

I've never carved my name on anything. But judging from what I've seen on the picnic tables of the West, there are many people who have. I've been tempted, all right. It would be great to come back to a place in ten years and see my name where I carved it a decade earlier. But I wouldn't carve up a picnic table. Chances are good it would get moved or be painted in a few years.

I could paint something on a huge rock, and if the paint was good, the message might last ten years. Nobody is going to move a big rock. Another place would be a high water tower. You see a lot of graffiti on those things. But I'd have to climb up very high— probably at night—and I might fall or get arrested.

A good place to put a message would be on a fallen redwood tree. At Calaveras Big Trees State Park in California, you'll find fifty-year-old carvings on one fallen tree. Redwoods take forever to decompose.

This all seems very destructive, and it is. But this sort of thing is nothing new. It's been going on for a long time. The American Indians, for example, carved and painted on rocks. Dozens of state parks, national monuments, and roadside markers preserve (and showcase) these petroglyphs and pictographs. American trappers carved on rocks and trees as they explored the Wild West.

The most expressive messages are those of recent times—the ones written in public bathrooms. Most of the authors, though, aren't interested in bringing anyone back in ten or twenty years to prove they were once there. It wouldn't be impressive.

No American highway is more famous than Route 66. Even though it was finally bypassed by Interstates in 1984, the road from Chicago to Los Angeles is fondly remembered by Americans who once drove it or knew it from song, literature, or TV.

Route 66 began as a series of cattle and wagon-train trails. By the early 1900s, the twenty-four-hundred-mile route was named the "National Old Trails Highway." In 1926, still mostly dirt and gravel, it was renamed Route 66. Paving was completed in 1937.

During the next half century, millions of Americans followed the road west. John Steinbeck immortalized it in his 1939 book, *The Grapes of Wrath.*

If you drive old Route 66 from Oatman to Seligman, you should stop and talk with the locals. Each person has a story to tell of the day the traffic stopped—when the Arizona stretch of the mother road was replaced by Interstate 40.

Ray and Mildred Barker, owners of the Frontier Cafe in Truxton, remember the day well. One day, business was so good they could hardly keep pace with it. The next day, practically nobody showed up.

"It was kind of like turning the spigot off," Ray recalled. "It

Ray and Mildred Barker, Frontier Cafe, Truxton, Arizona

was a relief at first, but after about two weeks we wished some of the traffic would come back." The Barkers laid off their employees, tightened their financial belts, and managed to hang on. Last year, before the Historic Route 66 Association of Arizona began promoting the old road, the Barkers were ready to give up. But they didn't, and business is gradually improving now as motorists rediscover the historic route.

Angel Delgadillo of Seligman was born along Route 66, a block from his present-day barber shop. He's the president of the Historic Route 66 Association of Arizona. He thrives on the attention it's brought the road, and even himself.

"I think I've lost a few customers because they got tired of hearing about Route 66," he said.

Delgadillo remembers how he and his brothers watched the Okies pass through town on their way to California. The cars would be packed with children and family possessions. Strapped to the sides would be a water bag and a mattress or two. Angel and his brothers would joke about the mattresses; one mattress meant the Okies were poor; two mattresses meant they were rich.

Some of the Okies' cars broke down in Seligman and their owners never left. Others earned some money, fixed the car, and headed on west.

Beatrice Boyd owns the Mobil station in Peach Springs. She and her husband opened it in 1948, when Route 66 was busy. Today, past normal retirement age, she still runs the two-pump station, even though her husband died years ago. She sometimes closes up during the middle of the day when she needs to run an errand; if someone needs gas there's another station up the road.

She doesn't stay in business for the money; it's just that she doesn't know what else she'd do. She hasn't ordered postcards or any automotive accessories in ten years. Dusty old fan belts hang on the wall; postcards show Route 66 when it was a main road.

Stephanie McPherson, Miss Route 66, is one of the few young people you'll meet along the route. As Miss Route 66, she gets to ride in a parade once in a while. Monday through Friday, though, she commutes from Truxton to high school in Seligman. It's ninety miles round-trip—all on Route 66. By the time she graduates, she will have driven the equivalent of twice around the world on the old road.

There's more to Route 66 than its old pavement.

Clark Gable, Carole Lombard, and twenty burros have something in common: They are the tourist drawing cards in Oatman, a semi ghost town west of Kingman on the original Route 66.

Oatman was once a town of eight thousand to twelve thousand people, depending upon which tourist brochure you read. Today, a few hundred people are left and the main industry is tourism. The main attractions are Room 15 of the Oatman Hotel, where Clark Gable and Carole Lombard spent the first night of their honeymoon in 1939, and the twenty burros that roam the streets begging food from tourists.

Oatman visitors can shop in about a dozen small stores, most of which sell regular tourist stuff. But while outdoors, they will often be hounded by a herd of hungry, bossy burros seeking a snack (merchants sell packets of burro food for twenty-five cents). On my visit, the critters were blocking traffic about a mile west of town. A motorist yelled, "Don't eat my Suzuki" as a burro nibbled on his parked car.

While the burros appear tame, they are wild animals. Local residents pet them, and visitors do, too. But the Oatmanians know

69

the proper way to do it; the tourists often do not, resulting in an occasional whack from a burro's rear leg.

So, if in Oatman, feed from the front.

Now, about Gable and Lombard. In 1939 they were secretly married in nearby Kingman after a three-year romance. They didn't tell anybody until the next day.

The newlyweds took Route 66 to Oatman, where they checked into an upstairs room of the two-story adobe hotel—the only two-story adobe building in Oatman (even today). Room 15 is small and plain with a white dresser, double bed with blue spread, and a few throw rugs over the wood floor. A single light bulb hangs from the ceiling.

Fifty years later, the room is preserved as it was that historic night. You can see it for fifty cents. Chicken wire covers the open door, so you can look but not touch. There are big poster-size photos of the two stars on the walls.

About a half dozen other rooms have displays of Oatman's history, but none is as interesting as Room 15. You can't stay at the Oatman Hotel anymore; try the Z-Inn up the street.

The hotel's bar is interesting. There are hundreds of one-dollar bills tacked to the ceiling—and even some bigger ones—including a hundred-dollar bill. Most are signed and dated, one by Ronald Reagan. "It might have been someone named Ronald Reagan, but I don't think it was *the* Ronald Reagan," the bartender explained. A married couple from Bullhead City sipped on Budweisers. "We put a bill up there in 1959, but we've never been able to find it since," the man said.

There are a lot of good sayings up on the wall. My favorite was PLEASE BE PATIENT. I HAVE JUST TWO SPEEDS AND IF THIS ONE ISN'T FAST ENOUGH FOR YOU, YOU SURE AS HELL WON'T LIKE THE OTHER ONE!

Other than the twenty burros, the famous bedroom, and the hotel bar, Oatman doesn't have much in the way of terrific attractions. But as western ghost towns go, it's pretty good—mainly because it isn't overly commercialized like Virginia City, Nevada, or Tombstone, Arizona.

But when it comes right down to it, the burros are the best thing about Oatman.

*   *   *

Casey O'Sullivan was tending Ed's Camp, a run-down junkyard/museum/rock shop and campground along the original Route 66 about twenty miles west of Kingman. Two fellows from Wisconsin were nosing around, looking at this and that and laughing. "I've never seen so much junk!" one guy said.

Ed Edgerton founded Ed's Camp in the late thirties, when the narrow road out front was the main route between the dusty Midwest and the promised land. Edgerton pumped gas and fed folks whose engines in Model T's and A's needed to cool a while before heading up Sitgreaves Pass to the west. While they were there, he sold them fire agate, a local rock that's beautiful when all polished up.

Clark Gable and Carole Lombard dined with Edgerton on their way to their honeymoon night at the Oatman Hotel. Comedian Eddie Murphy stopped by a couple years ago. "I think he was looking for a gold mine," said O'Sullivan.

Most people today just stumble on the out-of-the-way place. "They ask you questions about all kinds of things, then they don't buy anything," he complained. A money box by the guest register solicits donations.

O'Sullivan runs Ed's Camp with his mother Ruth. Only about a dozen other people live in the immediate area. Otherwise, it's just jackrabbits, coyotes, and a lot of snakes. "Sometimes the snakes come up to the back door of the house," said O'Sullivan. "They're trying to get warm. I wish I had a license for snakes. I'd have a few in here right now."

O'Sullivan, twenty-seven, is a holdover from another time—a jack-of-all-trades. He was born in Arizona and ended up at Ed's Camp nine years ago after working a few years in Laughlin, Nevada, for Southern California Edison. "They had a big explosion and a few guys got killed, and I said, 'Heck, I'd rather be poor than dead,' so I moved over here." He worked for a fellow named Keith Gunnett (Ed Edgerton had died years earlier). Gunnett, in his late fifties, taught the young man everything he knew. "He'd say that if you just knew one thing, then when that was gone, you wouldn't have anything."

Today, O'Sullivan tends to customers, dispenses soda pop at the snack bar (when it's open, which is only occasionally), and fixes water pipes, the tin roof, and about everything else. He arranges

71

and rearranges antiques and rocks and even sweeps the dirt floor.

He said he couldn't bear to live in a city. "There's too many crazy people there. They're always shooting at each other. There's crazies out here, too, but at least you know who they are." He said he stays at Ed's Camp for months on end without leaving—fine with him.

He remembered being in a traffic jam once. "It was some-where in southern California. I don't remember the name of the freeway. We went about one car length in ten minutes." At Ed's Camp, a car passes by every few minutes during the busy season.

I asked him if he were far from home and had to describe Ed's Camp to somebody, how would he describe it. He thought for a minute, then he answered: "A rock shop."

Truth is, there are lots of rocks at Ed's Camp—mostly fire agate, but others, too. Rockhounds would probably like this place. But about half of Ed's Camp is junk, or antiques if you want to be polite. There are rusty Acme and Eastside beer cans, and old bottles of Thrill and Kist soda pop. There are rusty stoves, rusty shovels, and beat-up bus seats. A 78-rpm recording of "Ragtime Cowboy Joe" by Dick Jurgens and his orchestra is four dollars.

The closed-up Kactus Kafe is next door. O'Sullivan took me through so I could see the four-door antique icebox. There's no price tag, but if it were in a shop in the California gold country, it would cost a bundle. O'Sullivan told me the inventory at Ed's Camp comes from "accumulation."

As I was getting ready to leave I asked O'Sullivan about the tree out front with all the soda pop cans hanging from the limbs. He said it got killed by lightning a few years back so they hung up the cans to make some extra shade. After hearing that, I didn't bother ask-ing my last question—if Ed's Camp gets hot in the summer.

Casey O'Sullivan doesn't have the market cornered on junk. Most humans have plenty of junk. I sure do. And, like most Amer-icans, I have a special drawer reserved just for junk—a junk drawer.

In the motor home I have two such drawers, one official and one unofficial. Junk drawers are for the things in life that defy categorization. We can throw something into this drawer and for-get about it.

At home, I also have a junk closet. It, of course, is for larger junk. I know from memory what it contains: an old lamp shade, a battery-powered golf game that I never played, a thirty-year-old life jacket, a broken vacuum cleaner, a broken electric heater, and a pair of wing-tip shoes. There are at least a hundred other things, none of which I will ever need again. To be honest, if that closet would disappear my life would be better.

The junk drawer in my motor home is tiny—nine inches square by four inches deep. This is a very small space, so you might think that the junk kept there would be important junk. But it isn't, and that's the point of a junk drawer. Nothing in a junk drawer can be important. If it were important, it would be in a drawer with important stuff. A junk drawer contains things that are too worthless to use, but not quite worthless enough to throw away. It's a never-never land for the miscellany in our life.

Here are a few of the things in my motor-home junk drawer:

- a four-inch round green badge that says TEMPORARILY IRISH
- an M. Hohner Golden Melody harmonica *in case I get bored and decide to learn to play it some day*
- a tiny plastic bag containing a nut, two washers, and one bolt
- one Wet-Nap Moist Towelette
- a blue Duncan Yo-Yo
- a book of matches from the Union Hotel in Occidental, California
- A Garbage Pail Kids' key chain with the words UP CHUCK

Those are the important things. There are several dozen other items, from a golf ball to an old tube of lip balm to a clothespin. There are also thirty-three rubber bands.

Now, I could throw away everything in this drawer and not suffer any noticeable loss. But even if I did, it wouldn't matter. The drawer would soon fill up again with new junk. Everybody needs junk. That's the way it is.

For a peek at the future, visit Arizona in the winter. Hundreds of thousands of retired folks migrate here annually seeking sunshine, shuffleboard, and conversation. They bathe in hot mineral pools by day, and they square dance at night. In between, they trade stories about aches and pains and grandchildren.

Walk past their houses and you may hear a Glenn Miller tune playing from the stereo. Peek inside and you will see five-by-seven photos of grandchildren, and a French poodle asleep on the couch.

This is the future for us baby boomers, who have only recently acknowledged that we, too, will grow old. Soon, the eldest members of our group will become senior citizens. Millions will soon follow. The America of 2010 will look very much like today's "snowbird" season in Arizona.

One difference, of course, will be the music. Instead of Glenn Miller it will be the Beatles and the Beach Boys. The tune "Little Old Lady from Pasadena" will take on a new meaning.

Pete Harrison works two days a week in an eight-by-fifteen-foot cage at Nick's Self Serve on Pima Street in Gila Bend. He takes motorists' money for gas, and sells cigarettes, candy bars, motor oil, and whatever else is for sale at Nick's, where the restrooms are advertised as clean but are not.

He says he spends five hours a day at his forty-six-foot trailer home, which is time enough to sleep. But mostly he drinks coffee and socializes at local cafes, which means shuffling between three spots in Gila Bend, population eleven hundred.

Harrison has lived fifty-five of his sixty-four years in Gila Bend. Since his divorce twenty-three years ago, he's lived alone. His oldest daughter is close by; she works for the Gila Bend Post Office.

Pete remembers when Gila Bend was bigger, when the population was twenty-five hundred—back when the railroad stopped in town, and before the two-lane highway was replaced by four-lane Interstate 8, which bypasses the town entirely. "There used to be twenty-seven gas stations here," he said. "Now there are six."

Except the two days he works, Harrison takes it easy—trying to keep away the loneliness. He quit drinking alcohol fifteen years ago, so he doesn't go to bars, which would be a logical spot to pass some time in an outpost like Gila Bend. "About all there is to do around here is drink coffee and smoke cigarettes," he said from his cage at Nick's.

One place to dine in Gila Bend is the Space Age Coffee Shop. It's next to the Space Age Motel, and right on the main drag. I was in the mood for cow, so I ordered a Space Burger Deluxe for $4.20.

Pete Harrison, Gila Bend, Arizona

It was the first Space Burger I had ever ordered in my life. It soon arrived, complete with fries, which turned out to be barely adequate. The burger itself was one third of a pound, with a slice of tomato and four pickle slices, but it was not at all juicy. Its aftertaste lasted eleven minutes—which is not good. I figure that the worse the burger, the longer the aftertaste. A good burger's aftertaste lasts no longer than three minutes.

The best things about the Space Age Coffee Shop are the pictures of planets on the wall, and the good postcard rack. Another interesting attraction is the local Rotary Club calendar up on a wall. It lists birthdays of many of the town's eleven hundred residents. On the day I visited, Mike Tworek was celebrating.

Last Friday night, in Willcox, I listened to the last two minutes of the high school football game on radio station KFM. It was an exciting finish as the Willcox Cowboys tried to score against the Thatcher Eagles. But the Cowboys didn't make it, and lost 8–0. It was a tough loss because, according to the radio announcers, the Cowboys have been a powerhouse in these parts for a few years. At the final gun, the radio announcers said they would be back with a recap after some commercials.

In a big-time game, you'd get statistics about who scored, how many yards the leading runners rushed, and what percentage of passes the quarterback completed. But in Willcox, on KFM, you don't get such precise statistics. The announcers said they figured the Cowboys' downfall was that they threw "five, but maybe six" interceptions, and that the leading rusher "*probably* didn't get more than fifty yards." That was it for stats.

A few days earlier in Gila Bend, a page-one story in the *Gila Bend Sun* was headlined MONSTER FOOTBALL (the local team is the Gila Monsters). A subheadline said ANTELOPE 41–GILA BEND 13. Here's how the story began:

> The season didn't get any shorter as the Rams from Antelope butted and bloodied the Gila Monsters during last Friday's game at Antelope. There was a lot of support for the guys from Gila Bend as the band and the cheerleaders made a bus full of noise. The band got into the swing of things early when they played the national

anthem after the local school had a recording problem.

Gila Bend had all scores by Bobby Calvin. The offense and defense played well at several turns, but the intensity was not sustained to a degree to effect [sic] the final outcome.

The story concluded with this comment about the next game against San Pasquale: "PREDICTION—Monsters win by a close game."

There it was in Willcox—a gumball machine that charged a penny. When was the last time you bought anything for a penny?

I've had my eye out for penny merchandise, and I haven't found much. Of course, you can buy a nut or bolt in a hardware store, but that doesn't count. So far, I've found a penny pony ride (plastic pony) in Hotchkiss, Colorado; penny candy at Golden Gate Mercantile in Ferndale, California; and penny Tootsie Rolls in Cohone, Colorado. There are still penny slot machines in Reno, but only in a few out-of-the-way casinos. Some very small towns still have penny parking meters. But not many.

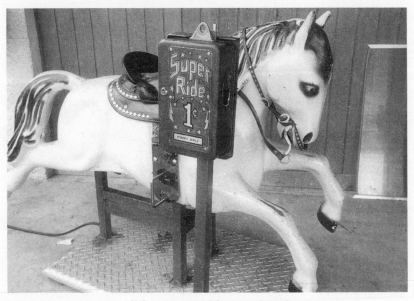

Something a penny will buy in Hotchkiss, Colorado

Pennies are so worthless that many stores have a dish with pennies by the cash register. If you come up short, you can take a penny from the dish. Some customers don't want pennies for change, so the clerk puts them in the dish.

Thoreau, in his book *Walden,* used the phrase "A penny for your thoughts." I don't believe he originated the saying, but back in his day, a penny was valuable, and could probably even have bought a thought. Today, you would have to offer someone a few bucks for their thoughts. Try offering a lawyer a penny for *his* thoughts.

Kids will pick up a penny from the ground because to a child a penny is money. Adults, even those poverty-stricken, won't pick up a penny at their feet because it's too much work and it won't buy anything anyway.

I suspect most stores don't sell penny merchandise for several reasons. First, there's no merchandise available. Second, even if there were, there's no profit in it. And third, what if a kid comes in to buy one piece of penny candy? It probably costs two cents just to ring up the cash register.

I awoke this morning at 7:30 A.M. to a parade of cars passing by my penthouse window. By penthouse, of course, I mean the upper bunk over the cab of my mini motor home. That's where I sleep.

I'm camped at the Justin RV Park near Tucson. It's maybe a twenty-minute commute to downtown. I figured the people passing by my motor home were commuting to work from their travel trailers. That isn't unusual. A monthly space here is $210, which is $7 a day. That includes your space plus electricity, water, and sewer.

Whenever I camp in an urban area I see this: people using small recreational vehicles as homes. Most do it because it is the only way they can afford to live. A home is costly in most places, and these folks aren't the kind who can come up with a ten-thousand-dollar down payment.

Some of these people are working temporary jobs, and the trailer makes sense. It's cheap living, and when the job ends, they can move on.

The couple camped next to me work on weekends. They have

a twenty-four-foot Open Road motor home that's probably twenty years old. On Friday nights, they leave this campground and drive to a nearby flea market where they spend the weekend selling stuffed pillows.

Marty Murphy, formerly of Lander, Wyoming, came to Arizona a year ago to hear the Pope speak. He never left. Today, he lives in a twenty-eight-foot travel trailer that he bought for $750. He gets free rent for keeping an eye out on a campground in Ajo, population twenty-three hundred.

With a gleam in his blue eyes, Murphy talked about the Arizona sunsets that he's seen from his campsite alongside a deep copper pit in Ajo. He pointed to a nearby mountain and recalled a storm that passed through a few days earlier. A huge cloud had wrapped around it like in a scene from the Bible.

His little trailer is a cluttered home in miniature. There's a refrigerator as big as most house models, and a stove, electric toaster oven, double bed, bathroom with toilet and shower, and a dinette that seats four or sleeps two. He named his trailer Casa Paloma Blanca, which means "house of the white dove."

Marty Murphy, Ajo, Arizona

At age sixty-eight, Murphy reflected about his life. "I wish now I had had a family," he said. "I know that's the most beautiful thing in life. You should get married and have kids. The most important thing is to share your life with others—but you may not know that until too late."

He talked about his big brother, who died recently. "You know he was never the kind of guy to let you know his feelings, but the day before he died, he told me he loved me." He paused to wipe tears from his eyes.

Murphy went to college in Washington, D.C., but found no job that required a college education, so he spent his life doing clerical jobs of one sort or another. "I was never a star," he said, but he smiled when he said it, like it didn't matter.

Today, in his spare time, which is plenty, he makes rosaries. "I just give them away," he said.

Arizona birds are the bravest birds in America. In the last two days I have nearly hit three of them. They flew across the road, directly in front of my motor home. If I hadn't slowed down, they would have been bird meat.

God, I believe, designed birds with automobiles in mind. The feathery things are adept at dodging vehicles in nearly all situations. They seem to know the right moment to avoid smashing into your windshield, but still fly close enough to scare the hell out of the driver. It's just my opinion, but I think birds enjoy this version of the "chicken" game.

Chipmunks, too, were engineered with automobiles in mind, but with unfortunate results. When a chipmunk spots an approaching car, it immediately streaks with bullet speed across the road to safety. Then, for some unknown reason, it fulfills some subliminal suicide wish by turning 180 degrees and rushing back onto the highway—just in time to be squashed by a Goodyear radial.

Buzzards, crows, and ravens, of course, are thankful for such behavior, for the fatally flattened rodents provide many a tasty lunch, sometimes cooked to beak-watering perfection by the hot asphalt.

When you put on as many miles as I do, you become concerned about hitting critters like birds and chipmunks. I do not, however, mind hitting insects, although they do mess up the windshield.

A reader once wrote to me with a suggestion on how to avoid hitting birds. She said her husband was an airwatch reporter in New Jersey, and that he always kept his helicopter's landing lights on when he flew. "Try that to avoid hitting birds," she advised.

While I felt it was a good idea, and might save a bird or two's life over a year's worth of trips, I told her I couldn't do it. My problem is that the Dodge doesn't have landing lights. I will be sure to order them on my next rig.

Here is a road game you can play that I invented. All you need to play are two people and a filmy windshield.

To start, each player draws a circle on the windshield with his finger. You can draw a small circle or a large one. The size of the circle will determine odds. The object of the game is to see in which circle the next bug will splatter. The player with the larger circle will have twice the chance of winning, so his payoff should be half that of the player with the smaller circle.

Bets can be made in money, or in cups of coffee at the next cafe. I prefer wagering on coffee.

This is a terrific game that makes bug-kills more meaningful.

There's a pack of coyotes howling outside my door as I've never heard coyotes howl before. They're a few hundreds yards away. It may take a sleeping pill to deal with all this racket.

Every year you hear of somebody losing his dog to a coyote. This happens once in a while in Death Valley. A guy ties up his poodle outside at night, and a coyote wanders in later and dines on the morsel. In the morning, the camper finds nothing left of Pierre but his leash.

Campers should keep their animals in sight. Coyotes figure a French poodle is a tasty change of pace from a jackrabbit.

A question has been going through my head for a few days now. It has to do with cows. I was wondering if they ever die of old age. Have you ever thought about this? If so, I'll bet you wonder, too.

Cats, dogs, horses, and parakeets die of old age, but I don't think cows do. I say this for a few reasons. First, cows have big appetites, so their food costs a lot over a lifetime. So who wants to keep one around if it costs a lot? Second, cows do not make friendly pets, so why keep one around if it doesn't even wag its tail when its name is called? Third, cows are raised for two purposes: meat and milk. Old cow meat tastes terrible, and an old cow doesn't give milk.

Now that I think of it, cows are a lot like NFL running backs: They lose their value with age.

My guess is that fewer than 1 percent of cows die of old age.

I get flack all the time from people because I think cows are dumb. They write to me and say that cows are not dumb at all. Some people tell me how they grew up with cows, and how they were like pets.

But, you know, I can't buy it. I'll bet I have stopped fifty times along the road to try to visit with a cow. I walk up slowly and say "Nice, bossy." All I want to do is pet its wet nose. Yet every time I do this, the animal will take a look at me, pause for several seconds while its microbrain processes the information, and then gallop away like I'm going to butcher it. Do you understand why I do not respect a cow for its intelligence?

Now you take wild burros, for gosh sakes. They'll come right up to me. And they are wild animals, not domestic ones like cows! They are smart enough to know they might get a handout, and they are usually right. I carry carrots and apples expressly for this purpose.

So don't tell me that a cow is anything even remotely intelligent. I have stated before that a cow's intelligence is perhaps 1 or 2. I'm willing to admit that the most highly evolved cow may have an I.Q. of 5, but that's tops.

I like cows in burgers and I like them in steaks. But I do not think they are smart.

A few hours ago I was speeding along Highway 77 toward Globe. I had spent a few minutes checking out Dudleyville, but it was a dud like its name, so I headed up the road to Winkelman, but it didn't interest me either. So I moved on.

Then something very strange happened: *I thought I had en-*

THE BEST FROM OUT WEST

tered the Twilight Zone. A few miles out of Winkelman, I turned on my radio, and guess what it was playing? The "William Tell Overture"—the theme from the *Lone Ranger.*

So there I was, speeding along a beautiful two-lane highway by the Gila River, and the late afternoon sun was turning the hills golden brown, and the saguaro cacti were backlit, and the "William Tell Overture" was playing on the radio. It put me into a dreamlike trance. I was expecting the Lone Ranger and Tonto to come riding around a bend. I looked up on the steep cliffs beside me, and I thought I might see an Indian brave on his pony.

But there were no Indians—only cacti, dirt, sagebrush, a broken yellow line down the middle of the road, and a sign that said DRIPPING SPRINGS WASH.

All the while, the "William Tell Overture" was playing, and my foot was getting heavy on the accelerator, and "Hi Ho, Silver" was on my mind. I was going forty-five, then fifty, and then fifty-five. I was a mad motorist in a trance.

Then from out of nowhere I saw something brown. It wasn't a horse—it was too big for that—but it was big and brown and coming fast. *Tonto?* I squinted my eyes, and suddenly it took shape.

A UPS truck.

What a disappointment! But the Lone Ranger music was still in my head, and I knew something else would happen. I just knew it!

Then—*it did*! I turned another corner and right by the side of the road was an amazing sign: ENTERING THE TONTO NATIONAL FOREST.

Something was going on here. I didn't know what, but I knew there would be something else up the road—something to do with cowboys or Indians. I was in the Twilight Zone—*I was sure of it now.* But what lay ahead?

Then, the "William Tell Overture" was on its last bars. Surely, if something was going to happen, it had to happen soon! It had to!

And, do you believe this? Just at that very moment *something did happen!*

It came from ahead—way ahead—from around a bend in the road. It was coming at me very fast! Our paths would meet in perhaps thirty seconds. My heart was going *pitter-patter, pitter-patter* at an alarming rate; I was pressed against the steering wheel, inches from the windshield, staring ahead—trying to see more clearly. But whatever it was, it was still too far away to identify. All I knew was that it was approaching very fast, and it was big and powerful and—yes—I suspected it *was indeed Indian!*

Then, just like that, we met and it passed in a huge blur. The music finished as the object raced toward Dudleyville.

I shook my head and slapped my face *just like in the aftershave ads,* and reality reared its ugly head. My trance was over. I had not been in the Twilight Zone after all. I was as disappointed as a motorist can be.

You probably want to know what I saw—what I thought was something Indian. Well, I'll tell you what I saw: I saw something big and long and fast and powerful. And yes, in case you're interested, it was indeed something (sorta) Indian. Out there, on Route 77, in the wilds of Arizona, on that day in October, I had an encounter of the automotive kind with—*a Winnebago.*

CHAPTER THREE

COLORADO

THE Yellow Jacket Post Office in Yellow Jacket, Colorado, opens promptly at 9:36 A.M. You read that right—9:36.

Here's why.

When Postmistress Lolita Aulston took over as postmistress in 1983, her higher-ups wanted her to open six hours a day Monday through Saturday. But Aulston told them six hours on Saturday was too much; she'd be twiddling her thumbs with little business. How about four hours on Saturday?

Fine, said her bosses, but she'd have to make up the two lost hours. So Aulston began opening Monday through Friday at 9:36 A.M. instead of 10 A.M. The extra twenty-four minutes, five days a week, equals two hours.

That's why the Yellow Jacket Post Office opens at 9:36 A.M.

*   *   *

I've been on the road so long I've forgotten what it's like to live in a real house—to have a stove with burners I don't have to light, a microwave oven, and a bed that isn't reached by aluminum ladder. I've also forgotten what it's like to have a shower with an unlimited water supply and a television that always gets reception.

I'm not complaining, mind you, just observing.

The weather person on Channel 8 in Grand Junction, Colorado, has just reported that "softball-size" hail fell earlier today in Dallas. Softball-size? Do you know how much such a chunk would weigh? A lot. It could kill a horse, not to mention a Girl Scout or two.

I'm thinking of conducting an experiment. I will write up a phony news story and mail it to the Channel 8 weatherman and to eleven other TV weatherpersons. It will say watermelon-size hail fell in Baggs, Wyoming. Of the twelve weatherpersons, my guess is one or two will report the news. "Believe it or not, folks, watermelon-size hail fell in Baggs, Wyoming." That's what they will say.

Of course, hail of such magnitude could only occur when the waste-water holding tank of a Boeing 747 accidentally lets loose at thirty-five thousand feet. Such hail would be "wading-pool–size."

I stopped at the cemetery in Delta, Colorado, to check out the community time capsule and its monument. The capsule was entombed July 4, 1976, and will be opened July 4, 2076.

I kept reading that last date—2076. I figured I would be 129 years old. This thought went through my head: *Chuck, you'll be dead as a doorknob—baking in some pine box—when they open that thing.*

So how can I ever learn what's inside if I'm six feet under? That thought made me mad. I wanted to see the contents of that time capsule. I felt like getting a pick and crowbar and opening it up right then and there. After all, I couldn't count on showing up in eighty-eight years. For gosh sakes, I'd be 129 years old!

Well, I worked out my frustration by thinking that there probably wasn't anything important in the time capsule anyway—probably only a local newspaper, a box of Coco Puffs, and a picture of Jimmy Carter. Who cares? So I walked around the cemetery and talked to the inhabitants. I had a short discussion (one-way, of course) with Ruby May Stanford, who left Planet Earth in 1924.

She won't be around either to see the time capsule. She and I—we'll be up in the sky, floating on a cloud, doing a jig, talking about what a drag it was to have to brush your teeth every day. Those twenty-first-century saps down below can eat their futuristic hearts out.

Speaking of heaven, I recall something I learned early in life. Like all little kids, I was curious about the hereafter. I had heard things in church, but I still wasn't clear exactly where heaven was or what you did there. For the answer I went to a reliable source: my mother.

I didn't ask her to actually define heaven, only to confirm my idea of it. "Mother," I asked, "do they have electric trains in heaven?"

She answered yes, and told me that little boys could play with them whenever they wished. It was a wonderful answer—exactly the one I had hoped for. For years after that, I did not fear death.

It was only after my hormones changed, and girls became more important than American Flyers, that I wondered if perhaps there was more to heaven than three-inch wig-wags and papier-mâché mountains. I concluded that heaven would be better if there were women to chase and parties to attend. Although I never believed this was all there was to heaven, the idea was reassuring.

A few years ago, when my aging hormones dipped to their third half-life, I again rethought my idea of heaven. Chasing women and attending parties, I thought, seemed too much work. I concluded that heaven would be fine if there was a good library, a full-time masseuse to rub my back, and reruns of *Hopalong Cassidy*.

Baseball fans considering the hereafter may wish to consider purchasing a plot in the Oak Creek, Colorado, cemetery. It looks directly over center field on the local high school baseball stadium. A long homerun could end up on your spot.

The cemetery, by the way, is worth stopping by if you pass through the town. It's full of interesting inscriptions on headstones, plus some photos of the departed. It's up on a hill, so there is a terrific view of the surrounding countryside.

At this very moment, a lightning storm is passing over the cemetery. Bolts of electricity are hitting around me. I'm in the motor home now so I won't get electrocuted. I hate getting electrocuted.

I was wondering, though, if birds ever get hit by lightning. I suppose they do. After all, planes occasionally get hit. I suppose if a bird gets hit there isn't much left. If you were on the ground below when it happened, you might see some feathers come falling from the sky. The poor bird would probably be vaporized.

I don't know why I thought of this. I just did. If you happen to know anything about this subject, please let me know. I like to keep up on scientific matters.

Where would Federal Express be if we were not all procrastinators? It used to be, if you needed something in New York by Friday, you raced around your office to get it into the mail on Tuesday evening—to be sure it arrived on time. Now, you wait until about noon Thursday, because you know that if you send it Federal Express it will be delivered—guaranteed—the next morning. Of course, putting a letter in the mail costs only a quarter; sending it Federal Express costs a lot more. The price of procrastination is high.

Sometimes when I'm waiting in line at a store and there is also a child in the line, I remember what it was like to wait in line when I was too short to see over the counter. I remember thinking to myself, as the clerk waited on the adults first and me last, that one good reason for growing up was to get decent service. I would be able to buy my red licorice without waiting. I vowed that when I became an adult, I would treat children as grown-ups—fast and with respect; in my line, at least, they would not be slighted. I have never forgotten that promise, and I keep it whenever I have the opportunity.

One vow I made, but did not keep, was always to dress in a youthful way. I made this vow in high school, when I first noticed how differently (and old-fashionedly) teachers dressed from students. One of my physical-education coaches, however, dressed very youthfully. "I'll be like him when I grow up," I vowed. I swore that I would never wear pants so long that they reached my shoes—and I would never—ever—wear shoes with rounded toes. My feeling was that teenagers were the most important people on Earth and I would always want their approval.

Of course, as I grew older I no longer felt a need to impress this group. I wore clothes that appealed to my new peers, former teenagers like me. Today, I wear clothes for their comfort value rather than their style. Three quarters of my wardrobe, I suspect, would make most teenagers gag.

So in keeping my youthful vows, I am one for two.

In my travels, I stop at every national park, national monument, state park, and museum that I can.

These visits have affected me in many ways, but in one way in particular: I have become acutely aware of time. I have become aware of how short a year is, or a decade, or a human lifetime.

When you visit a place like the Grand Canyon, you will learn that some of the land there was created hundreds of millions of years ago. Drive along the dry plains of the Columbia River in eastern Oregon and you will learn that the land was a rainforest millions of years ago. At Dinosaur National Monument in Utah, you will learn that dinosaurs existed for 125 million years. Yet we humans are labeled *old* when we have lived a mere sixty or seventy years. A fifty-three-year-old man I met last week told me that he had recently been addressed as "old man" for the first time. He wasn't happy about it.

The Earth has been here for billions of years and it will be here for billions more. How many human generations is that? Time is a relative thing. I'm a baby.

If I live to be eighty, I will have spent thirty-five years in bed. Frankly, I've got better things to do. Like drinking coffee, writing, driving my motor home, or taking a nice woman to dinner and talking about our failed relationships.

Thinking about the time I waste sleeping makes me mad. It's not the sleeping itself. Before you sleep, you have to get ready, which means brushing your teeth and changing your clothes. And getting up is even worse. You look like hell, with your hair all messed up, and there's stuff in the corners of your eyes, and you have *morning breath*. So you have to take precious time preparing yourself to look as good as you did before you went to bed the night before. Why not just stay up?

Some scientists say we sleep because when we were cavemen it was tough finding food. So we holed up in caves at night to conserve energy—so we could get by on less. I guess if you're in a dark cave there's nothing better to do than sleep. There was no TV back then, so sleep was logical.

But now we get plenty of food. Just look around. Half the guys in America over forty have bellies that sag over their belts.

And frankly, I've been thinking about what it's like to be asleep. You crawl into bed, close your eyes, and for the next eight hours trust God that Charlie Manson won't show up.

So I'd like to announce that I am not going to sleep anymore. I have plenty of food to eat, so I don't have to conserve energy, and I'm tired of getting into bed and then out of bed, and then having to wash the sheets every couple of months.

Sleeping is a pain in the behind, and I've already done it for about seventeen years, and that's enough as far as I'm concerned.

I'm going to spend my extra time learning how to tune up a Dodge.

Besides sleeping away seventeen years of my life, I've done a lot of other time-consuming things. I've spent:

- 1.5 months getting ready for bed
- 4 months getting out of bed
- 3.5 years at a typewriter or computer keyboard
- 1.2 years in a bathroom (shower time included)
- 4 days in pit-toilets (no showers available, of course)
- 1 month brushing my teeth
- 2.5 months combing my hair
- 4.7 years driving a car (based on eight-hour days)
- 4 months at stoplights
- 1.9 years eating
- 1.2 years on the phone
- 1 day at bank automatic-teller machines (recent development)
- 1.3 years watching TV news

- 1.8 years watching TV sitcoms
- 5 months complaining about something

All together, I estimate I've:

- eaten the equivalent of two cows just in *hamburgers and cheeseburgers alone*
- used enough shampoo to supply a typical girls volleyball team for two years
- devoured enough french fries to fill a Holiday Inn hot tub
- used enough toothpaste that if squirted in one continuous line would go from one Rose Bowl goal line to the other and back again—*twice*!
- driven the equivalent of a round-trip to the moon *plus* 8.5 *lunar orbits*
- drunk enough milk to supply Jackpot, Nevada, for 23 days
- eaten enough bananas that if laid end to end would form a curving line from one end of the Disneyland parking lot to the other
- used enough water washing my sheets and underwear to fill a Motel 6 swimming pool
- thrown away enough trash to fill a dump about the size of Gila Bend's

When you're a kid, Christmas comes once a year. When you're older, it seems like Santa's always at the mall. And birthdays—they're an eternity when still counted on fingers. When you're older, finish one cake and it's time for another.

My days (when I'm not traveling) seem like this to me: get out of bed, take a shower, eat oat bran, drink coffee for a while, write for a while, watch the evening news, go to bed, get up again, and take another shower. To be honest, sometimes I feel like I'm always in the shower.

I figure about the only way to make time slow down is to spend a lot of time in a dentist's chair.

Regarding time, I have a question. Why is it that time goes faster as we age? I don't know anybody my age or older who hasn't said to me, "Boy, time sure goes fast these days!"

Why does time go faster for a forty-year-old than a twenty-year-old? Why does time go even faster for a sixty-five-year-old? Does it have something to do with our experiences? Does it have something to do with routine? Is it something biological?

Do you know?

Do you ever wonder about "the last time"? What I mean is, do you ever wonder about when you will do something for the very last time in your life—take your last swim, go out on your last date, buy your last car, see a parent for the final time?

I don't mean to be morbid, but it's something I sometimes think about. I'm happy to think about it because it makes me appreciate everything I experience; you never know if it's a "last time."

Our first times are easy to pinpoint—a first date, first kiss, first job, first car. But we seldom recognize our last times until years after they happen. Many of us have said good-bye to a grandparent, only to realize later it was for the last time. We have kissed a lover for the last time without knowing it was the last time.

I already know of some things I have done for the last time. I've fought my last forest fire, dated my last college cheerleader, and written my last story on a typewriter. I've played my last game of tackle football, and performed my final trumpet solo. There's a good chance I've driven my last 1958 Volkswagen.

I have not eaten my last Cheez-Its. I'm pretty sure of that.

Peter Sullivan and his wife Lori Biggins-Sullivan invited me to their home for brunch this morning in Cedaredge, Colorado. I had met Peter the day before at his Roundhouse Books in downtown Delta. He started the business two years ago, after working in construction. He's doing better all the time, although building a book business in a town of only a couple thousand people is a slow process. But Peter seems satisfied.

Lori works in a home studio making pottery: vases, plates, bowls—that kind of thing. She wholesales her beautiful work to tourist shops. Her most popular item is a ceramic egg separator (it separates the white from the yolk). She's amazed at how well it sells. The only thing she can figure is that people buy them as gifts "for the person who has everything."

When I meet nice people like Peter and Lori, I don't want to leave. I wish they could be my neighbors.

Saying good-bye to people I meet on the road is the hardest thing I do as a part-time nomad. I meet people nearly every day—on the street, in a cafe, and at night in a campground. The campground meetings are the most meaningful because there is time to talk by a campfire for hours. We can be strangers at 7:00 P.M., and then like friends at midnight. A bonding occurs that would take weeks or months at home. Perhaps because we know we will never see each other again, we express feelings from deep inside, with no fear of having to explain them again later.

I have left these campfire chats feeling sad—knowing that in the morning the closeness will be gone. It is as if both parties will awaken with their emotional faucets once again shut. Guts have been spilled, and now it is time to move on.

It takes a toll on me. Each friendship leaves me a little more emotionally drained and often a little more lonely. That's why I have to return home every so often. There I can be with people whom I don't have to say good-bye to.

We should never underestimate the value of a friendship. If you have never thought about the word *friend,* you should; it is a word to be reserved for special people, not for just anyone. If you have one friend, you are lucky. If you have two, you are even luckier. Many people, I suspect, do not have one friend. And remember that it is never necessary to say "good friend," for a friend is always good. There is no such thing as a casual friend; they are only acquaintances.

A friend accepts you for who you are, for better or worse, and receives the same in return.

A friend is a blessing.

Cedaredge is the home of the biggest ice cream cone that I have ever seen, much less eaten. It's so big that if you buy two, you'll need a trailer to hold it all.

I exaggerate, of course. But a Tony Scoop is the most gigantic ice cream cone I have ever seen in my life, and that spans more than four decades and approximately 732 ice cream shops and 63 Thrifty Drug Stores.

It weighs in at one pound and one ounce, and is a sight to

behold. Its head server is Tony Mercep, with able assistance from wife Pat and mother Dolly. They are the proprietors of the thirty-four-space Aspen Trails Campground, gift store, and regionally famous ice cream shop.

"We started selling ice cream to bring people into the gift shop," explained Tony. "Now we take in more money on the ice cream than we do from the campground or the gift shop." Indeed. On Sundays, the biggest day, customers line up out the front door. Five hundred gallons go out during an average week—more in the summer.

Hired help is needed on hot weekends. But training is a problem: It's not easy to make a Tony Scoop. Hours of practice are needed.

The huge ice cream cone is served in dramatic fashion. The area behind the counter is hidden, so customers can't see it being prepared. First-time customers are astounded at what they see. When mine arrived, I said, "You're kidding," and Tony said, "No."

After thirty minutes, my entire chocolate Tony Scoop was making its way through my guilt-ridden body. I took a walk later to shake off a few of the million calories I had taken in. All the while I kept thinking, *Two more points of cholesterol, minimum.* But it was worth it for $1.85.

It's nearly impossible to describe a Tony Scoop. The best description came from a local newspaper reporter. He wrote, "Imagine eating a bowling ball on a cone."

So this is what it's all come to: staying out of the sun and not eating food that tastes good.

Last year, my dermatologist told me that some of the spots on my skin I thought were freckles were actually spots of sun-damaged skin. This morning I noticed a small patch of such skin on my face. *Sun damage*, I thought, horrified.

Then I looked outdoors—sunshine—beautiful, warm, gorgeous sunshine—*perfect tanning weather!* Spend a little time basking in it, then return home in a few weeks to foggy Sacramento and impress my friends with a tan.

Sure, and impress them with more damaged skin on my face! Used to be, people would say, "Ah, what a nice tan you have." Now they say, "Hey, fool, don't you know sun is bad for your skin?

It causes cancer." I tell them everything causes cancer. For Pete's sake, a couple years ago there was a story making the rounds on how radon gas was seeping out of our showers. So taking a shower could even cause cancer!

In my twenties, I would stay in the sun until I burned. I snow-skied in March without sunscreen, then came home the color of a lobster. I'd have a George Hamilton tan by mid-June.

And my wonderful diet! I miss it so. I would gobble down french fries, double cheeseburgers, Kentucky Fried Chicken and pepperoni pizzas—not once in a while like now, *but all the time*! I would pile sour cream on my baked potatoes. I drank whole milk and mixed real cream in my coffee. My favorite food of all was Kraft macaroni and cheese—the food choice of bachelors everywhere.

Now, except when reviewing a small-town cafe, I seldom eat anything fried; when I do, I feel guilty. I don't eat cheese, which I crave. I drink only skim milk—the blue beverage. I avoid anything with palm oil or coconut oil.

Conversations with my friends have changed in the last few years. Used to be we'd exchange stories about our love lives. Now we compare cholesterol counts.

Life is hell when you become responsible.

I turned forty a while back. Readers twenty or thirty will think of me as an older fellow, and readers sixty and seventy will think of me as relatively young. But that's irrelevant to what I really want to write about: my eyesight.

My closeup eyesight is deteriorating. It happens to a lot of people at around age forty and I'm no exception. I have always had this plan that I would never get old, but it's happening nevertheless. Technically speaking, of course, I have a few years to go.

My failing eyesight annoys me. I first noticed it was deteriorating about a year ago, when I couldn't focus on my shoulder. This came as a great shock, for I had always been able to see my shoulder clearly. I owned a parakeet for years, and he would sit on my shoulder. I would talk and he would chirp and everything was right with the world. Now such a bird on my shoulder would be a colorful blur.

A couple of months ago I was giving a special woman friend of mine a good-night kiss and I noticed that she was out of focus. This was annoying, for I prefer my women in focus. Later, I was eating a sandwich, and as I prepared to bite into the meal, I noticed it, too, was out of focus. I also prefer my food in focus.

These days when I read something I pick up the reading material and move it to my traditional reading range. But then I must adjust it away a few inches to make up for my deteriorating eyesight. This is a movement that I have always associated with older people. Now I am one of them.

Physically, I would say aging is not a particularly pleasant experience. Luckily, however, our minds seem to improve. I figure if they had beauty contests for minds, anyone younger than fifty wouldn't stand a chance, me included.

Saw a Popeye cartoon today. I couldn't wait for Popeye to get into trouble and then eat some spinach. Sometime during that cartoon, I realized that for my entire life I have associated spinach with strength. I've always disliked spinach, even though I can remember my mother's words from long ago: "Eat your spinach. It's good for you. It'll make you strong."

Every Popeye cartoon I ever saw reinforced that message. Too bad I could never acquire a taste for the stuff.

There are many other foods that could use Popeye to help their image. Prunes come to mind. If Popeye had gobbled a few prunes every time he got into trouble, prune sales would be a lot better today.

I woke up this morning to the soothing rhythm of hoofbeats as a man rode by on a horse. I closed my eyes and savored the sound. *This*, I thought, *is what civilization sounded like long ago, when there were no engines accelerating, no horns honking, no tires squealing, no DC-10s powering overhead on their way to thirty-five thousand feet.*

It was a pleasant, relaxing sound, but it only lasted a few minutes. A car drove up and suddenly it was 1988 once again.

I've shopped at my first Wal-Mart. It reminded me of K Mart, except there were no blue-light specials.

My first Wal-Mart was in Glenwood Springs, Colorado. I bought a videotape of an episode of Abbott and Costello, shampoo, and a light bulb. Wal-Mart did pretty well by me. When I got back to my motor home, I glanced at my receipt. Right at the top was the "Signoff Receipt" of the clerk who had just left the cash register. So I read on, proceeding to learn some trade secrets.

The clerk's scanning percentage was 90.63 (I guess this means the price scanner worked on about nine out of ten items). She signed off at 4:27 P.M. after averaging 10.83 rings per minute. Imagine: about every six seconds she rang something up on her register (No.1, by the way). So not only did I get to shop my first Wal-Mart, but I got to learn some trade secrets. It was a super shopping experience.

When you travel a lot, you sometimes forget what day it is. Most of the time it doesn't matter. But sometimes it does. Like today. I plopped three quarters in a newsrack for the Sunday *Denver Post*. Unfortunately I forgot it was Saturday, not Sunday, so I paid seventy-five cents for a twenty-five-cent newspaper.

Swap Shop is on the air on KRAI radio in Craig, Colorado. A man just called about his lost poodle. Before that, a woman was selling her guinea pig. Also advertised were a hydraulic log splitter, a 350 Chevy engine, a ton of hay, two geese, two baby goats, three yearling bulls, a miniature dachshund, and a "nice-looking duck." One woman wanted to buy some hay and two women were looking for laying hens.

Swap Shop is a regular feature. Chuck the announcer said it is on the air "come rain or nuclear attack."

It's 9:40 A.M. I have showered, eaten a bowl of Grape-Nuts, and downed my second cup of caffeine-rich coffee, my drug of choice. It is now time to secure the hatches of the Dodge and hit the long and winding road. Today's journey will begin here in Craig. I will stop first at the Safeway for supplies, gas up, then proceed north on what looks to be a lonely highway—State Route 13. The first organized civilization along the route is forty-one miles away—Baggs, Wyoming. After that, I'll follow alongside

Muddy Creek for fifty miles to the town of Creston. I don't know where I'll go after that.

This day has the makings of a lonely one. I expect no McDonald's or airwatch planes en route. Film at eleven.

The Safeway Satellite Network, Denver Division, was playing over the public address system at the Craig Safeway store. "We want to be your favorite supermarket," the announcer said. He also talked about Safeway's friendly employees and great service. And when he was done, music started playing again. I guess Safeway has these networks all over the place. The last one I heard was from the El Paso Division.

I was the second person in the checkout line at Safeway, waiting patiently for my turn. Then, behind me, another clerk came up, grabbed the cart of the person behind me (third in line) and led her to his register: "May I help you over here?" he asked as he pulled her cart. Meanwhile, I remained waiting in line.

It made me mad. This happens to me much too often. That checker should have asked me, not the person behind me. I had waited longer than she had. But he didn't. Is that fair? Write your congressman.

At the checkout counter, a feminine computer voice sounded out the price of each number as my checker Norm passed merchandise under the scanner. I asked Norm if he hears the voice at night in his sleep. "Oh, no!" he said, adding, "I love her. She keeps me straight. If I make a mistake she lets me know."

It was interesting that Norm had such an emotional reaction to his computer's feminine voice. It reminded me of the only computer voice I have any attachment to. It's the one I get every time I use my telephone calling card. The voice says, "Thank you for using A T and T." No matter where I go, she always says that. That computer lady and I have a good relationship.

In the Safeway parking lot, I overheard one woman tell another about a mutual friend, "It's the first vacation she's had in forty years." I thought about that. Imagine, one vacation in forty years! What a shame, with all there is to do and see in the world, that so many people can't get away. We should make some time for vacations. Even if it's hard to do so, we should make some time.

I filled up at the Texaco station in Craig before leaving town. I chose the self-serve pump, as I always do. I like to pump gas—the fumes are terrific. They cause cancer, but I like to live dangerously.

The only attendant was underneath a car doing some repair work. When I was finished pumping, he got up promptly to help me. He called me "sir" three times, and thanked me at least that many times. He was a nice guy, probably in his early twenties.

I was getting ready to file my cash receipt when I noticed that he had hand-written a personal thank-you note right on the top. Wow! Even though he was busy, he took the time to thank me in a personal way. I can't remember the last time a gas station attendant went to so much trouble to say "thank you."

I'll go back every time I'm in Craig. I support people who appreciate me.

Why is it, I sometimes wonder, that I feel guilty when I pass by a hitchhiker? It happened again today. A fellow was thumbing a ride just outside Craig. I just drove by. I looked in my rearview mirror after I passed and he was staring at me with a look on his face that said: *Why didn't you pick me up?*

Maybe he wasn't thinking that. Maybe I imagined it. I didn't owe that guy a ride. I'd be crazy, actually. There was a story in the newspaper this morning about a couple of guys who escaped from a prison near here. Maybe he was one of those escapees.

Still, I have this little pang of guilt every time I drive by a hitchhiker. To minimize it, I always look away. At all costs, I avoid eye contact. I don't know why I feel this way; I just do.

One of the most useless inventions of all time was car fins. I remember when my folks bought a 1961 Chrysler Newport. It had a great neon-lit dashboard, but more important, it had great fins. *If only I could drive*, I thought. *I'd love to drive a car with fins.* Now, fins aren't popular at all.

A good game to play while traveling with kids is to count cars with fins. On a good day you may see a half dozen.

If you're a parent and into child abuse, make your teenage son or daughter drive a car with fins. It's legal torture that won't land you in jail.

While car fins are not among the greatest inventions, I predict carmakers will bring them back. Maybe in ten years.

CHAPTER FOUR

MONTANA, WYOMING

I STOPPED at the St. Regis Gift Shop in St. Regis, Montana, this morning to check out the LIVE MONTANA TROUT display as advertised on billboards along the highway.

What a disappointment! About a dozen trout are displayed in small tanks. One big rainbow trout can barely turn around in its space. All the fish look sick; the eastern brook trout was resting on the bottom of its tank, looking very terminal. The rainbow trout looked the color that trout look after they've been on shore for several minutes.

I left without buying anything; I didn't feel like supporting the place. It also bills itself as the largest gift shop in Montana, but I stopped yesterday at Lincoln's 10,000 Silver $, which looked much bigger to me.

They should put the trout back in a river and stock the tanks with goldfish. LIVE MONTANA GOLDFISH sounds good to me. I'd stop. I like goldfish.

My phone book back home is hundreds of pages. There are even two volumes—white pages and yellow pages. The folks in Hot Springs, Montana, don't have so many pages to look through when they need a number. The whole book has only six white pages. And in case you're interested, there are six families named Johnson, five named Craft, five named Brown, but only three Smiths.

One animal I don't see much is moose. I see lots of deer, elk, antelope, and cows (thousands of cows), but seldom do I see a moose. The other day, though, I saw two.

I was sitting at a picnic table in a campground near Yellow-stone, minding my own business, writing on my portable computer, when all of a sudden I heard an unusual noise in the woods.

What was it? I was the only person around, so it couldn't be a human. I searched for evidence, and guess what I saw? It was a huge mama moose and her moose-ette—just a hundred yards away and charging toward me like two wild bulls. It was a human-moose collision course if I ever saw one.

Within seconds, the two beasts were thirty yards away and still charging. So to protect my life (and my motor home, of course), I raised my hands and waved like a crazy man. I also screamed, "Hey, you two mooses, get outta here!"

Well, the wild animals saw and heard me, but only after they had galloped to within ten yards of my campsite! I was one scared camper, let me tell you! Anyway, after they came to a complete halt, they looked at me with strange expressions on their faces—a look I'd seen on moose on *Wild Kingdom.* So I knew what they were thinking. It was this: *What the heck is this strange-looking wimp of a creature doing here?*

That's what was going through their heads. But they didn't think for long, maybe ten seconds. After that, they raised up, scanned the forest, and then turned 45 degrees. Then they put the pedal to the metal and headed into the sunset (the forest, actually).

I watched them disappear, and soon went back to my work like nothing had happened. But first I wrote some postcards. "You

101

won't believe what just happened," I wrote. "I nearly got crushed by a couple of wild moose."

OK, so I exaggerated. Shoot me.

A plane just flew over as I was taking a walk. It's 10:15 P.M., and pitch black. All the campers around me have gone to sleep. I was walking out on a trail, and the Milky Way was filling up the sky. As I was listening to my Walkman stereo, up in the air comes a plane flashing lights and crossing the sky, interrupting my view of the Milky Way.

So I took out my silver-and-red flashlight, which is powered by a single AA battery, and I flashed it right at that plane as it crossed the sky and I wondered if there was anybody up there with their nose pressed to the window looking down at this huge expanse of darkness. If there was, I wondered if they saw my little flashlight.

I suppose that's a question I'll never get answered.

As I drive around the West, I wish I were a geologist. Every time you turn a corner there's another rock formation. Some are red, some are gray, some are flat, some are standing up on edge. I took Geology 1A in college, and can remember a little of what I learned, but not nearly enough to figure out what I see on my trips. I know if I knew more, I'd appreciate more.

It frustrates me. One of these days I'll get back into a geology class.

An eighteen-wheeler truck packed with chickens just passed me. There must have been a thousand chickens, all caged so tightly they couldn't move. Some were stuck sideways, others nearly upside down. It was a depressing sight. I know chickens are fairly dumb creatures, but having owned a couple as pets once, I know they are intelligent enough to know what's going on.

The chickens in that truck must have been suffering. I vowed right then and there to never eat another chicken, but I changed my mind a few miles later, when I realized that if I cut out chicken there won't be much left to eat, now that I seldom eat beef.

Seeing a sight like this is very upsetting because you know there is hardly anything you can do to make the situation better.

About fifteen years ago I owned a dozen chickens. I was living in a house on three acres, so there was plenty of room. I bought my hens at a nearby egg farm for seventy-five cents each. The price was low because the birds were past their prime laying days.

I transported them home in several tiny cardboard boxes. As soon as I arrived, I carried the boxes to the backyard and let the chickens free. What happened next is interesting.

Those chickens would not stand up! They just squatted there like there was a low ceiling over their heads. They stayed that way for a half hour before finally standing up. Once they got up, it took them a few more minutes to walk. After that, they were the happiest hens you'd ever hope to see. They just walked around in circles, and they clucked, and everything was right in their world.

I realized later that my hens had been imprisoned in tiny cages for their entire lives. They had never stood up, much less walked. They didn't even realize there was such a thing as standing up or walking.

It was a great feeling, knowing I had liberated those chickens.

I stopped by the Oxford Cafe in Missoula for breakfast. The eggs were fine, the hash browns were fine, but the brains were questionable.

The Oxford Cafe has been around for 105 years. Besides the dining section (just a counter), there's a bar, poker tables, keno area, and a few draw-poker machines (gambling of this kind is legal in Montana). Customers wear cowboy hats, and the cigarette smoke is thick. In the morning when you're eating breakfast at the counter, a few feet away a cowpoke might be downing a Moosehead.

The twenty-four-hour "Ox" is an institution in Missoula. Maybe your great-granddaddy ate there.

I stopped by for one reason—to eat some brains. BRAINS FOR A POOR MAN $3.25, it said on the menu. So that's what I ordered—with eggs.

Ten minutes later, the waitress slapped down an old white plate that weighed a pound all by itself, and was older than my great-aunt Fanny. It was all filled up with a pile of greasy hash browns on one side, two sunny-side-up eggs on the other, and brains—a huge heap of cow brains—spread all over the middle. It

103

was a lumberjack-size meal, with big ol' ugly brains as the star attraction.

I went right for the brains, depositing a large brown heap into my mouth, which, incidentally, was doing its best to stay closed so as to avoid accepting the cargo. But it reluctantly opened; strangely, at the same moment, my eyelids slapped shut to mask the pain sure to come from a taste as bad as a tastebud ever tasted.

Mouth loaded, I swallowed the first-ever brains to occupy my stomach—a historic moment. And guess what? *Those cow brains tasted swell!* So swell, in fact, that I harpooned a few more. I was proud of my courage as I devoured six more forkfuls. Then, as I prepared to swallow helping number seven, *they* sat down—*the two guys.* For the next sixty seconds, from their counter seats next to mine, they stared at my plateful of brains like there was nothing better to stare at in the whole Ox. "Don't hardly ever see anybody eating brains that way," one guy said. "Most people have 'em in scrambled eggs, not like you're having 'em."

Well, for Pete's sake, I thought, *if nobody eats brains this way, then why am I eating brains this way?* My own brain struggled for an answer. But before I could reach one, I felt a hundred eyes upon me from every corner of the Ox—all staring at the dumb tourist eating cow brains *but not in scrambled eggs like everybody else!*

I looked down at the remaining glob of meat on my plate, and what I saw was no longer just food. It was brains—ugly, brownish-gray *cow brains!* My appetite was gone in an instant. I tried to eat more brains, but it was no use. I couldn't. I picked at what remained, but finally rearranged them on the plate to trick the waitress into thinking I ate more than I did.

I was done eating brains for that day—maybe forever. And the brains already inside my stomach were speaking to me—growling, and threatening to return from whence they came. I decided right then and there: The next time I'm in Missoula, I'll order Pigs in a Blanket.

Eating those cow brains wasn't the best of all possible experiences; however, now that some hours have passed, I can report that they stayed down. So it wasn't such a bad meal.

As I drove away from Missoula, I was thinking about brains. I started off thinking about cow brains—about how big they are compared to how poorly they work—but then I thought about our very own human brains.

I have often marveled at how my brain can remember so many things. I usually think about this when I pull into a town I haven't visited for years. As I enter the city, I know what's ahead. My brain has remembered details like the location of a gas station, a cafe with good pancakes, a painted-up fire hydrant, or the route to a campground. I know where the men's room is at the courthouse. At the library, my brain remembers the location of the magazine rack—even before I walk in the front door.

All this information has been with me since my last visit, or from trips years earlier. That's amazing! Where does it store the information? How much space does it take? How is it that as I enter town, my brain can instantly open a file of information it recorded years before?

My computer mimics a brain, but its capacity and recall are vastly more limited. Every so often, I instruct my computer to "Empty Trash," which is its way of disposing of unwanted information. My brain never empties its trash. It just stores information one byte after another, year after year. My brain has already stored a trillion things and there is room for trillions more.

Information my brain has stored includes the location of a good newsstand in Roswell, New Mexico, and a restaurant with ten-cent coffee in Mount Shasta, California. My brain stores information about a bakery in Sisters, Oregon, and where to find a campsite in Quartsite, Arizona. My brain has a file for great highways and terrible highways. It stores millions of bytes of information about bad cafes and good cafes.

It even stores information about a sidewalk I roller-skated on as a child in West Covina, and it can recall the location of my locker in high school. My brain even stores details of a crawdad I caught thirty-three years ago at Buck's Lake in Plumas County, California.

My brain is a super organ.

Someone in a nearby campsite is zapping bugs with a 12-volt bug zapper. If you're an insect, you better stay away from this camper because any man who transports such a machine into the wilds is a man who celebrates death.

At home, he probably has a 110-volt zapper—a big-league

zapper for super kills. In the wilds, he brings along his compact 12-volt version. It packs enough punch to do the job, despite a diminished "fry-factor."

At home, the man has equal territorial rights with bugs. It's him or them. In the forest, the bugs' home, the man is a visitor, here for a day on his way to somewhere else. Yet his little green machine hangs from a pine tree and goes *keet, keet, keet* all night. Each *keet* represents a bug turned into carbon.

Scientists say insects will inherit the world after a nuclear holocaust. They can survive, humans can't. Men with bug zappers will be zapped. Bugs won't. Everywhere bugs will drink champagne and swap bug-zapper stories.

Hardly a day passes that I don't think about how wonderful it is to be on the road. I've been meandering around Montana for a couple of days, taking it easy, finding a few stories here and there, but mostly just being purposely lost. And I've been thinking again about how great a life this is, of how much fun it is.

It's good to be away from familiar places. It's invigorating to read different newspapers, to see unfamiliar faces, to turn corners on the road and not know what you'll find. It's fun to walk along the main street of a town you have never visited and peek inside the windows.

It's fun to stand in front of a small-town barber shop and watch the barber at work. It's fun to stop by the Rexall drug-store fountain for a tunafish sandwich and a chocolate malt. It's fun to talk with the waitress at the cafe on Main Street, and the old fellow with the stubby beard and no teeth who passes the time on a wooden bench in front of the Texaco station.

It's good to be alone (in moderation, of course)—with no telephones to interrupt your thoughts, and no responsibilities other than to yourself. It's wonderful to wake up when you wish, instead of by a rude alarm clock. It's good to know that you can go where you want, when you want. And it's terrific not to have to mow the lawn, take out the garbage, put on a tie for work, drive on a clogged-up freeway, or "do" lunch in a restaurant with high prices, ferns, and waiters who say "Enjoy." (I prefer a waitress named Betty who wears sneakers, chews gum, and calls me "honey.")

It's also fun to go into a small-town market and check out the prices. Take bananas, for example. A big supermarket may be charging forty-nine cents a pound, so you load up. Then you pull into some tiny store where the floor is wood and where there are no generic brands and only one checker—and you walk by the magazine rack, past the cashier to the small produce section and find a sign, BANANAS, 3 pounds for a dollar.

Maybe all this doesn't sound so great to you, but it does to me.

Bozeman has a terrific main street. I explored it today, not looking for anything in particular, just looking. Maybe you've heard the saying: "Sometimes I sits and thinks, and sometimes I just sits." Well, my saying goes like this: "Sometimes I looks for things, and sometimes I just looks."

Today, I was in the mood to "just looks." As it turned out, however, I did find some things.

The first thing I found was a huge pink pig on the sidewalk in front of the Brass and Wood Antique Shop. It was a six-foot fiberglass pig named Porky. Owner Bob Arnold told me he was getting ready to clone Porky into three more pigs, due to demand. He said they would sell for eight hundred dollars. So if you're looking for a big fiberglass pig, Bozeman would be the place to shop.

Porky got me so excited about pigs, I decided to eat pork for lunch at Pork Chop Johns, where a pork chop sandwich goes for $1.90. Pork chop sandwiches are popular in Bozeman, but even more so in Butte.

It was a hard choice, though, choosing between Pork Chop Johns and the Cowboy Cafe next door. I try to stop at any cafe with the word *cowboy* in its title; don't ask me why, because I don't know why. Anyway, my pork chop sandwich was OK but not totally wonderful.

After I left Pork Chop Johns, I stopped by the Powderhorn, an old-fashioned sporting goods store. Owner Bob Bradford explained why there were 250 stuffed animal heads up on the walls—including "Big Red," the last ox to pull freight over Bozeman Pass. He said a lot of local hunters shot the animals, had them stuffed, then took them home only to be greeted by their wives with "Not in this house. . . ." So they brought their trophies to the Powderhorn, where they went up on the wall.

The Powderhorn was selling Red Ryder BB guns, which was

very exciting to me because I owned one as a child when Red Ryder was my hero along with Hoppy and Roy Rogers. It was interesting how Daisy had packaged the gun. On the side of the box was this message: I'M RED RYDER. ASK YOUR DAD—HE KNOWS ME.

I'm glad Red Ryder is making a comeback. I hope he makes it to a miniseries. I'd watch for sure, even if I had to drive a long way to get reception.

So I have to say, based on seeing Porky, eating a pork chop sandwich, stopping by the Powderhorn, and seeing the Red Ryder BB gun, that my visit to Bozeman was a good one.

When you write a personal letter, you know that your words may not get read for a few days. I say this because I write a lot of letters. Sometimes I do not mail a letter for a day or two, often because I cannot find a mailbox. Then when I do, it may take one to three days for the letter to reach its destination. So my words may be five days old before they are read. A lot can happen in five days.

Sometimes when I sit down to write a letter I think I should find a phone and call. My message could thus be delivered instantly. But there is a reason why a letter is better than a phone call: A letter can last a long time and be read over and over again.

Take the case of my father. When he was away fighting World War II, his father wrote to him regularly. My father saved those letters. His father, sadly, died before my dad came home. Now, four decades later, those letters help me know a grandfather I never met. As I read his words to my father, I sometimes become so absorbed I believe he was writing to me. So I know my grandfather because he took the time to write.

A friend of mine has communicated for the last twenty years with a fellow he served with in Vietnam. Each has saved the other's letters. Sometimes they photocopy an old letter and send it back. These letters have thus become journals for these two men. Their written words have documented two decades of their lives— marriages, divorces, good times, bad times.

Writing a letter is much more than a cheap way to send a message.

*   *   *

Out here in the rural West I sometimes think about cowboys. I know a few things about cowboys because I watched a thousand cowboy movies before I was ten—Hopalong Cassidy, Roy Rogers, the Cisco Kid, Gene Autry—terrific guys like that.

Today I was thinking about the best scene in those cowboy movies, and do you know what it was? It was when the good guy was chasing the bad guy on horseback and he'd catch him on the ridge of a hill (never on a flat straight-away), and then he'd jump from his horse to the bad guy's horse and they'd fall off and then *roll and roll and roll down the side of the hill—all the way to the very bottom.*

It was that rolling down the hill that was so great. Just thinking about Hoppy or Roy rolling down some hill gets my heart pounding. I want to find a hill and roll.

But I'd get dirty. So I'd better not.

A while back, a fellow told me a story about Roy Rogers. I don't know if it's true or not, but if the guy was telling me the truth, then what I am telling you is the truth. If he was lying, then I am lying. So don't use this story for serious research.

The story the fellow (a journalist) told me was about a time he went to Victorville, California, to interview Roy. This was a few years back, long after Roy had retired from show biz. Anyway, the reporter got to Victorville, where he was told Roy was in the nearby hills riding a dirt bike. So the reporter drove there. He found Roy by his dirt bike, which he had crashed. Roy was so mad he was kicking the motorcycle and swearing to beat hell.

That's the story. No big thing, really, and maybe not even true. Still, I like it because it's so hard for me to believe. No matter how hard I try, I cannot imagine Roy riding anything but Trigger, or maybe another horse. I cannot picture him, one of my all-time favorite TV cowboys, riding a motorcycle. I cannot.

But even more incomprehensible to me is that Roy would ever say a bad word. In the hundreds of hours I watched him on TV and in movies, I never heard him utter even one bad word—not one! Therefore, I am certain that Roy does not swear, just as I am certain that his wife Dale Evans would never do a nude scene.

The more I think about the reporter's story, the more I think it isn't true. No, Roy does not kick motorcycles, much less ride them, and he does not swear. He doesn't. Period.

So never mind.

The weather is different in Wyoming from back home in California. One minute it's sunny, then the next there's lightning and pouring rain. Then, a half hour later, it's sunny again. Back home, storms are more consistent.

A few hours ago here in Rawlins, bolts of lightning were hitting less than a mile away. Everywhere I looked they were blasting from the sky to the ground. It was so noisy I couldn't hear the radio. One bolt hit a few hundred yards away. The flash and thunder came at the same time. The motor home shook like there was an explosion. It was scary. If I'd had a cat aboard, it would have been climbing the walls. Just like me.

I got a kick out of advertisements for two motels in Rawlins. The Golden Spike Inn advertises "Franchise Quality." The La Bella Motel advertises "Motel 6 Prices."

Does "Franchise Quality" mean it's supposed to be good? I guess "Motel 6 Prices" is an easy way to say "cheap rates." The motels in Rawlins are dirt cheap. One advertises rooms for twelve dollars, and others are about sixteen. Most of the places need paint or remodeling.

Rawlins is an outpost along Interstate 80. In the old days, when cars moved slower, it was probably a logical place to stop for the night. But nowadays, when vehicles commonly speed along the remote Interstate at seventy or seventy-five miles an hour, motorists can go on to a bigger city in a few hours—Cheyenne or Salt Lake City perhaps. Maybe that's one reason Rawlins looks like it's past its prime.

You've heard of two-headed monsters. How about a two-headed Cadillac? Coming or going, the 1955 Caddy outside Perkins Conoco in Rawlins looks the same. The car with two front ends has been parked there since 1966.

Folks stop by every day. They can't figure it out.

Robert Perkins and Jack Gunderson assembled it in 1962 out of two junked Cadillacs. Perkins owned the gas station; Gunderson owned a body shop. Ever since, the car has appeared in parades. People think it's funny.

It takes two people to drive it, according to Steve Perkins, Robert Perkins's nephew and the manager of Perkins Conoco. "The driver up front controls the throttle, gears, and brakes. The driver in the back just steers. One driver is facing forward, the other backward."

The only way to tell the actual front of the car from the back is by an automatic headlight dimmer device on one dashboard. When the car goes one direction, taillights show on the back. When the car goes the other way, the lights show on the other end.

The car can move the traditional way—front wheels first with back wheels following—or it can go nearly sideways. "It's great for parallel parking," said Perkins. "You just pull right up next to the spot and pull in." Perkins says the car "is not for sale at any price."

He said it was too good of an advertising gimmick. Yup.

The subject on the morning radio talk show here in Rawlins was women and stress. But only a few people called in. One woman said she wouldn't have as much stress if her husband would thank her once in a while. "I know he appreciates me. I just wish he would tell me sometimes," she said.

Another woman said her life is stressful because there isn't enough money to go around. "When your husband's making six or seven dollars an hour, that doesn't go very far when you're raising kids," she explained. A male caller said single mothers who raise their families alone feel the most stress. "A lot of the husbands around here have just taken off," he said.

Anyway, that's what three people had to say about women's stress in Rawlins.

For a stress-free occupation, you can't beat running a Kool-Aid stand. Of course, the money isn't so hot, and if you're over twelve years old people may think you a little strange for operating one. However, all in all, a Kool-Aid stand is the best business in the world. The cost of your inventory is zero (Mom supplies the product), and the cost of your location is zero (Mom and Dad supply front yard and card table).

You get to keep every penny you earn. You don't even have to pay for liability insurance or workmen's compensation insurance. And Uncle Sam doesn't ask for taxes.

We grown-up business persons should have it so good.

I'll bet many of today's successful business persons ran Kool-Aid stands as children. I, for one, operated one—selling Kool-Aid and sometimes lemonade. Actually, I sold whatever my mother provided; to be honest. I was more interested in profit than product.

I also cut and watered lawns and even baby-sat a kid named Earl. The baby-sitting job, although considered more girl's work back then, was OK, for Earl's parents always left plenty of candy—a fringe benefit a youngster could appreciate.

One of my profitable ventures was scouring new housing developments for soda pop bottles. Fred's Market paid me two cents apiece—good money. I put my earnings into a special fund. My plan was to one day buy my parents a swimming pool. We never had a pool, so I assume my earnings never amounted to much.

My first official job was in sixth grade washing dishes at the cafeteria at Merced School in West Covina, California. I worked for thirty minutes a day and was paid thirty cents. Every two weeks or so I would get a paycheck from the West Covina Unified School District. I'll never forget the day I got a whopper! It was $4.50.

Fremont County, Wyoming, is said to include the largest unfenced area in the United States—eighty square miles. When I read about it, it didn't seem impressive at all. Yet now that I think about it, nearly everywhere I go there are fences. Sometimes, on a lonely road, I feel like walking off into the countryside to snap a photo. Yet two times out of three, there is a fence in the way. So maybe eighty square miles without fences is a pretty big deal.

I hear a Rain Bird sprinkler. That means it is spring. In winter, nobody out West (except in Arizona and southern California) waters their lawn. The Rain Birds are silent.

Hearing a Rain Bird means that warm days have arrived. It means I can soon put away my heavy jackets and umbrella. It means I can soon sit outdoors until midnight. It means I can soon sleep with my windows open.

I love Rain Bird sprinklers.

*   *   *

A motorist on Highway 202 today really bugged me. He was ahead of me for about five miles in his Dodge Colt, doing about forty-five miles an hour. Well, that was too slow for me on that boring Wyoming road, so I passed him. The next thing I knew he was up to sixty and right on my tail. I couldn't figure out why he suddenly decided to speed up. He tailgated me for about five more miles, then decided to pass. After he got in front of me, he slowed down to forty-five again. I couldn't believe it. Thinking about that guy still makes me mad.

Speed is something relatively new to humans. A hundred years ago about as fast as anyone went was on horseback, perhaps at twenty-five miles per hour or so. Today, we routinely drive along at sixty-five mph on freeways. On the Concorde jet, we cruise at fourteen hundred miles an hour—twenty-three miles a minute—six football fields in the blink of an eyelid.

Actually, sixty-five miles an hour on the ground seems a lot faster than fourteen hundred mph eight miles up. That high, the ground doesn't seem to move. But at sixty-five mph at ground level we speed by trees and signs at an amazing clip. If you watch the pavement alongside your speeding car, you'll see only a blur. The eight-foot center line will look only a foot long—an optical illusion caused by our rapid movement.

Observing America at sixty-five mph is like viewing a movie from the back row of a theater. Details are missing. But slow down, and the details appear—the flowers on bushes, the peeling paint on buildings, the fast-food wrappers along the road.

Try this: Walk a street you normally drive. You'll be amazed at what you see—houses you never knew were there, names on mailboxes, flowers in bloom, curtains in windows, cracks on sidewalks, and maybe even the freckles on a child playing in a front yard.

We go fast today because we have the ability, even though we aren't always in a hurry. Maybe we should slow down once in a while to see what's there.

We all do this, even though we shouldn't: We go to the supermarket on an empty stomach. We end up buying things we shouldn't. I did it today here in Casper. And (wouldn't you know?) the first department I came to was the bakery. The smell drove me crazy. The cherry strudel looked and smelled mouthwatering, as did the Danish rolls, cake donut puffs, and the lemon jelly rolls. I hope nobody was looking at me, because I was drooling.

Using all of my willpower, I only succumbed to buying a bag of blueberry donut holes. Ten minutes later, back in the motor home, the bag was two-thirds gone. After that I didn't have to worry about lunch—the donut holes did the job.

Still, I was proud of myself for not buying more junk. When I go to a grocery store on an empty stomach, I'm asking for big trouble—usually in the form of the two "C's"—calories and cholesterol.

Boy, I thought the New Mexico winds were bad. I forgot how bad they get in Wyoming. The Casper winds are threatening to topple the porta-house. I'm considering devouring some seasickness pills. It's either that or a few shots of Jim Beam.

The wind is getting inside the motor home through the cracks. As I write, my computer is bobbing up and down just like me. The wind is getting on my nerves. I'm thinking about getting out of this state pronto—going somewhere with rain or snow or even "softball-size hail."

I hate being shaken against my will. It turns me from a nice guy to an evil monster—my personality, anyway.

Grrrrrrrr.

Sunset Boulevard is mighty wide. Antelope Drive and Palomino Avenue are also wide. Bar Nunn's town layout is odd. It doesn't seem normal, and it isn't. Bar Nunn was once an airport—Casper's Wardwell Airfield. Today, six miles' worth of three old runways and taxiways are the town's streets.

Bar Nunn, Wyoming, has about eight hundred residents. The only commercial establishments are a campground and a couple of small manufacturing companies. There's a city hall, complete with a mayor, city council, and supporting cast. Although there is no town jail, there's a tiny courtroom.

Bar Nunn was a busy place in the forties and fifties when it was Casper's main airport. Today, cars travel where DC-3s once rumbled. But once in a while, a pilot gets confused and sets down. Several years ago, two planes landed in two weeks. One of the pilots said he thought the airfield was still in operation. He told Bar Nunn officials he'd taken off from there forty-three years earlier. Pre–Bar Nunn days, those were.

I have crossed the Continental Divide about twelve times on this trip—four times today alone. It's a pretty exciting experience for a guy from California's Big Valley. Every time I cross it I want to stop to photograph the sign. But I recently stopped doing it. After you have about thirty shots of Continental Divide signs, you start getting bored. Your friends get bored after seeing the seventh or eighth photo. My big project now is taking photos of signs for lakes. I'm specializing in Fish Lake and Trout Lake.

I'm camped at the Indian Campground in Buffalo, Wyoming, across the street from the Super 8 Motel and next door to the Dash Inn restaurant. I may get a Dash Inn Burger for dinner.

I stopped here yesterday in the middle of a storm. I had planned to stay in Gillette, but it was raining terribly, so I decided to hop on the Interstate for Buffalo, sixty-five miles west. Twenty miles down the highway, the wind started. The radio announced that a tornado watch had been issued. There was also a possibility of damaging wind and hail. And there I was in the middle of nowhere, fighting the wind, which was blowing the motor home from one lane to another. Luckily, there was little traffic.

I kept checking the sky, looking for a tornado. I had my video camera close by just in case. I thought of Dorothy and Toto.

Anyway, I made it to Buffalo, and checked into the Indian Campground, which turned out to be a nice place—somewhat sheltered from the wind. So far today there is no wind. But it's only noon. It usually comes up in the afternoon. I can hardly wait.

Independence Rock is along Wyoming Route 220. This was one of the most famous landmarks along the two-thousand-mile Oregon Trail. Many pioneers signed their names or left messages for others on the huge rock. At one time as many as forty thousand names were visible; most are gone now, covered with lichen.

A small bridge leads visitors over original ruts from wagons that passed here between 1848 and 1869; most were on their way to the California gold fields. As I stood there, I tried to image wagon trains, horses, and people on foot passing over this exact spot 140 years before. There were no highways, no roadside rests, no Burger Kings or Motel 6's up the trail.

Many of those pioneers were headed for Sacramento, my home. For them, there was a month or two of hard travel ahead. Today, it takes two days. What a difference 140 years makes.

If you ever meet me on the road and look very closely, you will notice I have no hair on the fingers of my right hand. Yet I have hair on the fingers of my left hand. You may wonder why.

It's because I use my right hand to light the burners of my stove. About twice a month, my hand gets too close to the flame. Whatever hair has grown in the previous two weeks is burned off. It doesn't hurt, but it smells. The smell of burning hair is worse than the smell of a wet dog.

When I return home every six weeks or so, I'm always thrilled by my home stove, which lights without a match. It's very wonderful and magiclike. For the next six weeks, the hair on my right fingers grows back. I feel very handsome all over again.

Readers have advised me to buy those long matches you use at the fireplace. They have a good idea, but it wouldn't work for me for the simple reason that I do not believe in buying matches. Why pay for matches, when they're free in cafes and gambling casinos? In this day and age, with everything so expensive and with Uncle Sam taking more and more from us in taxes, why pay for something you can get for free? So what if I have to burn a little hair on my hand? Big deal! Hair grows back. Money doesn't.

Besides, I like reading matchbook covers. I like those ads about courses you can take to finish high school. Even though I've already graduated, I enjoy reading the ads. When you're out in the middle of nowhere with no TV or radio reception and no newspaper to read, you have to do something. I like to read matchbook covers. To each his own, is what I say.

I've had it with pioneer museums. I hope never to see another old plow.

But it seems every town has a pioneer museum. The people

who settled the West could never have suspected that their foot-stools, tables, stoves, and plows would be so fascinating a century later.

I figure in a hundred years, towns are going to want stuff from the good ol' 1980s for their museums. So they'll display black-and-white TVs, Sony Betamaxes, tubes of Preparation H, Honda three-wheelers, Vanna White dolls, Sears microwave ovens, hair blow-dryers, and Exercycle bikes.

The Exercycle exhibit will be very interesting. Here's what the plaque will say: MORE THAN THIRTY MILLION OF THESE EXER-CISE CYCLES WERE SOLD IN THE 1980S. EACH MACHINE HAD A SPEEDOMETER. AFTER EXAMINING THOUSANDS OF THESE DE-VICES, HISTORIANS HAVE DETERMINED THAT MOST MACHINES WERE NEVER PEDALED MORE THAN SEVENTY-TWO MILES.

The good museums will have an actual room from a McDon-ald's, complete with a statue of Ronald the Clown. A plaque will read: IN ONE SURVEY, THIS CLOWN HAD A HIGHER RECOGNITION VALUE THAN THE PRESIDENT OF THE UNITED STATES.

I wish I could be around to check out these museums.

I was thinking some more about the Oregon Trail. It was really a one-way street, wasn't it? The pioneers probably didn't have to pull over very often for wagon trains going in the other direction. Everybody just went west, just like Horace Greeley suggested.

One of the big news items around Wyoming these days is that a rancher near Cheyenne is fed up with the Air Force disturbing his cows to get to its MX missile silo. The rancher has accused the Air Force of trespassing. He claims his cows are so disturbed they're not putting on weight like they should; it's costing him a lot of money. The Air Force says it is doing nothing wrong.

The rancher says it wasn't so bad when the silo contained a Minuteman missile, but now that it houses an MX, the Air Force is showing up about forty times a day.

This is too much excitement for a cow.

Writing of cows and the government makes me think of coy-otes and the government. A few years back, the federal govern-ment funded a university study to see why coyotes liked to eat sheep. Do you believe it? I don't remember how much money they spent on the study, but it was enough to buy a good American car, or maybe a half dozen Yugos. Anyway, all they wanted to learn was why coyotes eat sheep. For gosh sakes, I would have told them the answer for ten bucks. Coyotes eat sheep because they taste good. Anybody knows that.

The farther I am from a big city, the more often I see couples sitting snuggled up in the front seats of their cars. Usually the car is a pickup truck with one long bench seat. In the country you often see couples sitting about as close as they possibly can to each other. The guy is driving and the woman is by his side—almost like they're glued. They're so close that if the stick shift is on the floor, the guy has problems getting into fourth gear.

Bench seats, like those in most pickups, promote close sitting. They are best at drive-in movies, where snuggling up is generally more important than the B-movie up on the screen.

Of course, eight of ten drive-in theaters you see are closed these days. Of the two still open, one's used as a flea market, and the other one still shows movies.

Drive-in movie theaters were great in their time, but they are dinosaurs now. Today's smaller cars are the reason. Volkswagen beetles and all the compact cars that followed did in the drive-in. Did you ever try to snuggle up across the parking brake in a VW bug, or in the backseat? How about in a Toyota Pulsar?

Going to the drive-in in such a vehicle means you have no choice but to watch the movie—a lousy idea because the picture and sound quality in an indoor theater is ten times better. But back when seats were larger you could do other things—social things, if you know what I mean.

Back then, young folks didn't have their own apartments quite so early in life, so the drive-in (or "passion pit," as they were sometimes called) was a good place to get a little privacy. Today, many kids can afford an apartment at age eighteen; those who can't can find someplace roomier than the backseat of a Toyota to do their snuggling.

When it comes to unusual hobbies, David Wimp of Riverton takes the cake. For seven years, the ex-army sergeant has been adding numbers on a calculating machine.

David Wimp, Riverton, Wyoming

He punched in the number *one* in 1982. Then he added *one* to that number, and *one* to that number, and since then has continued. When I visited him in mid-1989, the last entry on his paper tape was 2,644,862.

One bookcase is filled with rolls of calculator tape—five thousand numbers per tape. He has another bookcase ready for tapes to come. All together, his tapes add up to 47,574 feet—an incredible nine miles! He enters numbers every day. His best single day in 1989 was Sunday, February 26, when he punched in 7,070 numbers. He spends entire weekends at the calculator.

"My math teacher in high school told us that if we could count to a million in nine weeks he'd give us an A-plus," he told me. "I wrote down the numbers with a pencil but only got to twenty-five thousand." That was the start.

In 1982, he began counting in earnest—with a goal of one million numbers. It took him five years. Then his uncle showed him a shortcut on the calculator, and it took him only a year to enter the next million.

Why does he do it? "It's my hobby. I enjoy it," he said.

He lives off his army retirement pay and earnings from his part-time business, Wimp Lawn Service. He has only two regular customers, so he has a lot of time to sit at his calculator.

He doesn't use regular calculator tape, but makes his own. He prefers freezer paper from Safeway—the kind the butcher uses to wrap meat. He cuts it into strips, tapes it into a long roll, loads it on the calculator, and resumes adding numbers. He also uses colored paper he buys at K Mart. "I don't use black paper, dark blue, green, or red. The numbers don't print well."

He burns up calculating machines. "When I buy a new one if it breaks down within a month, I can get a new one free," he said. His favorite was a Texas Instruments model. But, like all the others, it eventually died. "I took it to be repaired and they told me I had burned up the logic board. So I told them to throw it in the dumpster." He also soaks up ink rolls—one for every fifteen thousand numbers.

He keeps track of his mistakes. As of my visit, he had made a total of 3,225 errors.

He can't envision a day when he'll stop adding numbers. His plan is to reach five million. But that's Plan B. First there's Plan A:

to count backward from three million to zero. "That'll be a challenge because I'll have to hit the subtract key instead of the add key," he said.

An ad on the radio today said that the average person smiles fifteen times a day. That figures out to about once an hour, considering nobody counts smiles while we sleep.

It seems to me that we could improve our world a lot if we would all smile twenty times a day. In the United States alone that would be about 1.25 billion more a day.

Picture this: a forty-two-year-old man, traveling from the California coast to the innards of Wyoming in a beat-up squareback Volkswagen. In the backseat are thirteen screaming kids with diarrhea.

Sound like fun? It happened to John Mionczynski, who conducts wilderness expedition trips using goats as pack animals. As far as he knows, he's the only one in the United States doing it.

He often has to drive long distances from home to buy a kid—like in the case above, where he picked up thirteen screaming infants in Eureka, California.

"They were fine when the car was moving," he explained. "They'd lie down and go to sleep. But when I stopped, they'd all stand up and that's when the diarrhea would hit. The smell bowled over one gas station attendant. She leaned into the window and all the goats stood up. The car picked up an aroma that hasn't left."

Mionczynski lives alone "in the suburbs" of the semi ghost town of Atlantic City, Wyoming. He's used goats for years to haul water to his utilityless cabin, but he first became interested in them as pack animals in the mid-seventies while studying bighorn sheep for the U.S. Forest Service. His packhorses couldn't keep up with the sheep. Goats could.

Female goats won't carry as much weight as the males, but they take great care with their cargo. "You can pack wine glasses or a microscope on the females," said Mionczynski.

Living with about thirty goats has made Mionczynski an expert on the animals. For example, he will tell you that goats make great pets, with some personality traits like a cat. "They're very

121

independent. When you call them, they may not respond. Ring the dinner bell, though, and they'll come immediately."

Mionczynski has learned that goats like music. "Not rock, but they love melodic tunes. If they don't like a tune, they'll walk away. But if they like it, they'll gather around in a semicircle, lie down, and go to sleep. When the music stops, they'll stand right up."

He said that his goats love it when he plays the concertina or Irish flute. When he stops playing, they'll walk up to him and bite his hand; it's their way of saying, "More, please."

When it comes time for a pack trip, though, the goats that are to carry the heavy loads will sometimes slip away to a back part of the pasture to hide. But once on the trail, Mionczynski said they eagerly follow along. "They look forward to going to new places and tasting new weeds."

What do you do when you buy a new car? For one thing, you trade in your old one. But have you ever wondered where your old car ends up? Used cars don't last forever.

One day, your old car will die. If it dies in the city, it will be hauled to a junkyard. But if it dies in the country, it will be hauled nowhere; it will remain where it dies—along the road, in back of a store, or in a front yard.

Travel the back roads as I do, and each trip you will see thirty dead deer, sixty dead jackrabbits, three dead coyotes, thirty-four dead snakes, twenty-three dead squirrels, seventeen dead skunks —and six thousand dead cars.

I think in fifty years people will consider our present-day automobiles primitive. If you really think about it, they are already primitive. But they're the best thing we currently have for personal transportation.

They are very noisy, especially when they are not running well, and they pollute the air. Some scientists say we are experiencing a "greenhouse effect" in which the Earth's temperature is warming, thanks in part to auto exhaust.

Cars are also unsafe. Every day people crash in them. Hundreds of those people die. Others survive and spend the rest of their lives in wheelchairs. Still, we drive, because there is nothing better than a car for going where you want, when you want.

Cars also break down a lot because there are so many moving parts. Automakers have improved the performance of cars through the years, but in doing so they have made them so complicated that a backyard mechanic can't do his own repair work anymore.

My old 1958 Volkswagen was a bit more powerful than a go-cart, but I could do a lot of the mechanical work myself. Now, with all sorts of sophisticated electronic gizmos, you need a Ph.D. in mechanical engineering to figure out what to do when something goes wrong.

Someday they'll look back at our slow, gas-eating, polluting vehicles and laugh—sort of like the way we think of Stanley Steamers today.

Speaking of the greenhouse effect, I have some disturbing news. While we have all been busy blaming this phenomenon on humanmade pollutants, some scientists say it could be caused—at least in part—by gas from cows. Do you believe that? The scientists say there are so many cows on Earth these days that their gas is helping destroy the ozone layer around the planet.

The average cow, it is said, produces several hundred gallons of methane gas a day. Considering all cows in the world, this adds up to billions of gallons of gas—smelly gas, I might add.

The more I learn about cows, the more I'm glad I'm not one. If you are a cow it is like this: You're confined to a boring, sometimes freezing-cold pasture for a few years, belching and passing gas, and then when you get fat some guy comes along and herds you into a truck stuffed with a bunch of other fat and gassy cows, and then you all stand around with dumb looks on your faces and belch as you are driven to some pen. There you stand in mud and manure until somebody mercifully turns out your lights. After that, you're chopped up into pieces and shipped in an ice-cold truck to a McDonald's or Safeway. And then people eat you—rare, medium, or well.

To top it off, even when you're alive, you're so stupid you never know what's going on. And now we learn that as long as you're alive, you're contributing to the greenhouse effect.

I should ask Dick Hegg, the owner of the Longbranch Saloon in Luning, Nevada, about cows. He owns one named Friday. The animal was born twelve years ago in a cattle truck parked across the highway. The truck driver didn't want the calf, so he asked Dick if he wanted it. Dick said yes, and Friday has been around ever since. There have been times, said Dick, when Friday has wandered into the bar and up to customers, licking each as an introduction.

I wonder if Dick knows that his animal is contributing to global warming?

Thirty years ago, Norma Brunski hung a sign outside her King Cole Liquor Store in Kemmerer, Wyoming. WHERE THE LADIES CAN SHOP, it said.

"It's a good advertisement to bring in the ladies who don't like to go to a bar," said Brunski, who runs the combination bar/liquor store with her son and daughter-in-law, Pinky and Evelyn McPhie.

The ladies of Kemmerer still show up at King Cole Liquor for a drink and maybe to watch a soap opera on the big-screen TV. "In some bars, you get unsavory characters who might put the make on

Norma Brunski, Kemmerer, Wyoming

you. We don't allow that here, so those people don't patronize this place."

When she isn't serving drinks or ringing up the cash register, Norma is often off fishing or hunting. At 11:00 A.M. when part-time employee Betty Baxter shows up, "I take off fishing with my two dogs," she said. She also hunts, and has even bagged two moose. Asked how old she is, Norma balked. "Just say I'm as old as my teeth and as young as my mouth."

King Cole Liquor is located on the town triangle in Kemmerer. Some folks say the reason Kemmerer has a town triangle is it's too small to have a town square.

I was listening to a tape today of some old sixties music— "Dead Man's Curve" by Jan and Dean, and "Surfer Girl" by the Beach Boys. I was wondering if I'll still like listening to this kind of music when I'm eighty. Will I still enjoy "Be True to Your School," "Earth Angel," and "The Little Old Lady from Pasadena"?

Today, if a group of older folks gets together, they might play a Benny Goodman, Frank Sinatra, or Andrews Sisters record. I can't imagine that in thirty years a bunch of my friends would want to listen to "Teen Angel" or "Surfin' Safari." I bet we will, though.

And what about the distant future? I wonder what it will be like in a million years to look back at a Frank Capra movie or an episode of *Alf*.

What will future humans make of Archie Bunker, Vanna White, and J. R. Ewing? Will they find Barbra Streisand attractive? What will they think of the movie *Bedtime for Bonzo* starring Ronald Reagan? Will they enjoy reruns of *The Newlywed Game*? Do you think they will be interested in taped highlights of the 1989 Super Bowl?

Today, we can look back only seventy or so years in film and even less in TV. Yet, we can already see changes in society—hairstyles, automobiles, clothing, language—and attitudes. Twenty-five years ago, married couples on TV still slept in twin beds.

I can't conceive of humans being around in a million years. I wish I felt differently, but that's a long time for a complex and often violent world to survive. Still, we humans are an amazing bunch. Optimists will argue that whatever problems come along, we will solve them. I hope so.

The dinosaurs, after all, lived for 125 million years. Of course they didn't have an A-bomb. But if we humans do survive, what a wonderful thing it will be for our descendants to see how we lived in the twentieth century. It would be like us watching people from the Stone Age. Do you suppose Elvis will still be popular?

Dallas Scher is a real-life wrangler who was born too late. He was living and traveling in an eight-foot pickup camper, along with his companion of one year, Sharon Coffel, when I ran into him on his way from Apache Junction, Arizona, to the Triangle C Ranch in western Wyoming.

Dallas is an accomplished quick-draw artist, and the couple will entertain guests at the Triangle C Ranch. They already have an act: Sharon holds three balloons—two in her hands and one between her feet—and Dallas explodes them from ten feet away with special bullets in his .357 Ruger six-shooter. It's good he doesn't use regular slugs, because he's missed a few times. "It just stings," said Sharon.

At the Triangle C, Dallas will lead ranch guests on horseback rides and work as a guide for hunters in the fall. Sharon will cook, waitress, clean rooms—whatever needs doing.

They live in their tiny camper most of the year. There's a single-burner propane stove for cooking, an ice chest, a color television, and lots of cowboy stuff—bandanas, cowboy boots, saddles, and special rope for Dallas's rope tricks.

"Who needs anything else, when you're outdoors all the time?" asked Sharon, a divorcée from Michigan who spent thirty years waiting tables before running into cowpoke Dallas. The couple's wardrobe consists of Levi's, cowboy hats, and western shirts. Sharon carries one pair of tennis shoes for when she waits tables, but Dallas only has cowboy boots—seven pair. Everything they own is packed in their camper. "If I can't haul it, I don't want it," said Dallas.

"I tell people I was born a hundred years too late," he continued. "I should have been born in the eighteen-sixties or -seventies. But there are still places where I can take off on a horse and believe I'm back in that time. I'd rather sit on a horse on the top of a mountain, knowing there was nobody else around, than be sitting in a Burger King. There's no money, no future, no security, but I wouldn't give this up for anything."

126

Dallas Scher and Sharon Coffel

*　　*　　*

It seems that every few months I read another story about U.S. Highway 50 in Nevada. "The Loneliest Road in America" *Life* magazine called it a few years back, and now Nevada has posted signs along the way to capitalize on the publicity, hoping to pick up some curious tourists.

It's not true, really. U.S. 50 through Nevada is remote, but there are a hundred roads as lonely. Wyoming 220 is as lonely; so is Wyoming 28. Even Nevada has roads as lonely as U.S. 50—U.S. 6 and U.S. 93 come to mind.

Still, I love U.S. 50. But calling it the loneliest road is like calling Miss America the most beautiful woman in America. There are plenty of others—it's just that one happened to get judged in a contest.

The best thing about driving a lonely highway is you get a lot of thinking done. The idea for my newspaper *Out West* came to me on a lonely highway in Wyoming.

Today, in that same state, my mind was fertile. Thoughts popped into my head one after another. I noted each one in a small notebook, then wadded up the page in my left pants' pocket. After a few hours, my pocket was stuffed. When I have a bulge of paper in my pocket like that, I am a happy writer, and a happy man.

If I didn't have nerves of steel, I would be hiding under my dinette table at this very minute scared out of my wits—afraid that I was being invaded by monster insects. A giant moth—and I mean *giant*—just slammed its fat, fuzzy body against the window of my motor home, only inches from me as I typed on my computer. It made a huge thud, like a good-size dirt clod hurled by a mischievous child. It came back moments later, again throwing itself madly at the window, trying to get at my lamp. Its eyes reflected the light's glow, making them look an eerie orange color—ugly and monsterish.

It wanted in very badly, and it kept smashing against the window—over and over again, defying death, or at least a severe headache, in its passionate quest for my G.E. sixty-watt light bulb. It was a bug possessed if I ever saw one.

I wrote earlier about a man who transports a portable bug

zapper into the wilds, to kill insects wherever he goes. Frankly, I wish I had the machine at this very moment. This bug has got to go.

Dean Murkers is the entire population of Bill, Wyoming. The ex-mayor is also a part-time clerk at the Bill Store, the only retail business in town.

Murkers owned the combination store/post office for thirty-five years until he sold it recently to Webb Stoddard. Now he just works there six hours a week. Bill is north of Douglas on State Route 59, a highway lonelier than a Maytag repairman. The store is across the street from Dull Center Road.

Although the population is only one, it wasn't always that way. It was much larger twelve years ago: the population was five. Besides the Bill Store, there's a community center and a one-room school. Eleven children attend the school, which would include grades K–8 except there are no eighth-graders. So it's just K–7 this year.

Perhaps two hundred folks live within ten miles. The Bill Post Office has twelve boxes. Stamps, postcards, etc., are kept in five

(left to right) *Dean Murkers, Phyllis Johnson, and Webb Stoddard*
Bill, Wyoming

drawers behind the Bill Store cash register. You can go to the post office and buy a beer in the same spot.

The entire inventory of the Bill Store would fit in a corner of a typical 7-Eleven. You can buy a bag of Twin Bing candy for fifty-five cents, a quart of Quaker State motor oil for $2.15, or a pair of Tom Cat rubberized gloves for $3.99. And you can buy beer. "We couldn't stay in business if it weren't for beer," said Stoddard. You can buy a BILL YACHT CLUB T-shirt for $7.50. The best buy, however, is a half-pound hamburger for $2. It may be the best burger to be found along a lonely highway.

Phyllis Johnson is a Bill Store clerk and postmistress—except she isn't an official postmistress. "I'm the Officer in Charge," she explained. "The difference between that and a postmistress is about thirty thousand dollars a year."

The store is the gathering place for locals. Chuck and Rhonda Boswell live up the road. "We don't have a phone," said Rhonda. "We come here for news." Stoddard's son, J.R., was trying to decide whether to drive thirty miles over dirt roads to pick up some wool to be hauled. If it didn't stop raining, the wool would get wet. A fellow walked in with a frown on his face. The horse he was hauling had been hurt. He took J.R. outside for a look.

Not much goes on in Bill. About the biggest social activity is driving to Douglas, thirty-five miles away. By the way, Bill was named for a guy named Bill.

Demah Kern, mother of four and rural flagperson, was bundled up under a few pounds of rain gear, directing traffic at a soggy construction zone on lonely Wyoming Route 59 near Bill.

She's been flagging for six years. "I never get bored," she insisted. "I talk to the people. The most famous person I met was the Swiss ambassador to the United States. I was working on a highway near Yellowstone."

One time, during a thirty-minute delay, a couple got out of their car to square dance. "They said if they were going to be there that long, they should probably get some exercise. So they turned up their radio and danced."

Once in a while some guys give her a bad time. But she can handle them, she said.

Talking with Demah made me realize that the flaggers at construction zones are a different bunch from ten years ago. Back then, they were all guys. Today, they are at least half women, and many of those are senior citizens. It's not unusual to see a sixty-five-year-old woman directing traffic. Demah isn't sure why there are so many women flaggers these days, although she's willing to guess. "Maybe men feel it's a woman's job. They can make more money working on the equipment. Would you stand out here for eight dollars an hour?"

On this day, she would put in ten hours. Some days she works fourteen. "This is not what I want to do forever," she said.

So what does she want to do? "I don't know," was her reply.

Holy jackalope! The town of Douglas is the place to learn all about the legendary half-jackrabbit, half-antelope. There's even an eight-foot jackalope statue near the Texaco station; some local folks want to erect an eighty-footer out by the Interstate. It would be the world's largest jackalope, not to mention the world's largest fiberglass jackalope.

Douglas, like much of Wyoming, is still trying to recover from a depression since the oil-boom years of the early 1980s. About fifteen hundred residents moved elsewhere when the economy bottomed out. Today, some of the survivors think an eighty-foot jackalope visible from Interstate 25 would help. It would only cost $125,000 to build.

But even without the giant jackalope, Douglas, population about five thousand, is already famous as the jackalope capital of Wyoming, if not the world. Jackalope drawings and statues are on billboards, hotels, even on a park bench in front of the police department. A billboard outside town warns motorists to WATCH OUT FOR JACKALOPES.

The chamber of commerce sells plastic jackalope lapel pins for a quarter. They also issue official jackalope hunting licenses. Successful hunters, by law, must "report their kill to any tavern in Converse County, Wyoming."

Not far from downtown, taxidermist Jim Herrick makes and sells stuffed jackalopes. Herrick's uncle, Douglas Herrick, is credited with creating the jackalope's imagery in taxidermy and is said to be responsible for the creature's fame.

"One story I was told was that he came home from hunting

131

jackrabbits one day and threw the rabbits in a pile," recalled Jim Herrick. "One ended up right next to some deer horns, and it looked like the horns were on the rabbit. My grandmother named it a jackalope." Today, Jim Herrick sells hundreds of jackalopes a year. He'll probably sell a lot more if the city builds the giant jackalope out by the interstate.

Of course, the most popular story about the jackalopes goes back further than Herrick's uncle: In the 1800s, it is said, there were two kinds of jackalope—the kind we know today (the prong-horns) and a sabertooth jackalope. The mythical animals were famous for allegedly imitating human voices and carrying a tune. Their harmonies, cowboys reported, sounded much like those of Roy Rogers and Dale Evans.

Douglas is less famous for Tom Turkey. Yet you should know about this fowl, as he is a most unusual bird. Tom lives on Smylie Road with owners Jim and Bobbi Herrick and their two children Jeremy and Luke. The bird likes to follow the kids a half block to the school bus stop. There he waits patiently in line hoping for a ride. Of course, the bus driver always leaves the turkey behind, so the bird returns home in a fowl mood to try again another day.

When he isn't following children to the bus stop, Tom struts about his yard like a watchturkey, letting out an occasional *spifff* sound. You get the idea this bird would like to taste a little human flesh.

The day I visited, there was some talk about Smylie Road that perhaps Tom would soon be a father. But nobody was sure and the hen who might know wasn't cluckin'.

What's most impressive about Tom is his ability to belch. With a gentle squeeze of the chest by master Jim Herrick, Tom lets out a burp of monumental proportions—deep and loud, crude and tasteless—a redneck belch from a featherneck bird.

Tom will never be a Thanksgiving meal. "My wife would never let me butcher him," said Jim.

It should be noted that Tom is very ugly—at least by human standards. But perhaps he's a heartthrob to the females of his species.

We'll never know.

CHAPTER FIVE

OREGON, WASHINGTON

CAMPING in a remote and empty campground is good for me, even though I can be lonely in such a place. Perhaps, though, we all need some time like this, away from other people and the constant stimulation of our day-to-day lives.

For me, this is a time to recharge. My mind is almost forced to do some thinking beyond the call of duty. So I don't mind these times alone.

I tried my television last night and couldn't pick up anything. This morning I tried the radio, but only three stations would come in, and they were too weak to understand. There isn't a phone for at least ten miles, or a newspaper, so I'm stuck with myself until tomorrow morning, when I'll head up the road to Crater Lake National Park. So I'll just walk around, talk with the squirrels, and ponder whatever I feel like pondering.

I remember a few years ago when I was in a campground not too far from here, along the Umpqua River. As I pulled in, I heard on my radio that Princess Grace had been in a car accident. "But it appears she's all right," the announcer reported.

The campground was in a valley where the radio signals couldn't get in. So for the next two days I had no idea what was going on in the world, or how well Princess Grace was doing. When I got back on the road and in range of a radio station, the announcer was talking about her funeral preparations. What a shock!

Today, out of touch with the world, I wonder if I'm missing anything important. Probably not. But even if I am, it doesn't matter. I couldn't do anything about it anyway.

I was just thinking about how our lives are like football games. We go along with our day-to-day activities as if we have unlimited tomorrows. Then, one day, our time is up.

In football, each team plays the first fifty-eight minutes like the game will last forever. The trailing team figures it has plenty of time to score.

Then something happens to change everything: The two-minute warning sounds. Suddenly, the team that's behind accomplishes things it couldn't begin to do for the first fifty-eight minutes. It completes spectacular passes, kicks long field goals, makes terrific runs—and maybe even wins. Why does the team wait until the last two minutes to play this way? Why not do it the whole game?

It's the same with our lives. We just plod along figuring we've got an unlimited time to achieve our goals. Why not pretend our two-minute warning has sounded, and then live accordingly?

I'm going to try it. I'll let you know if it works.

I'm visiting the grave of Arthur B. Haley at the Mayville cemetery. He died February 4, 1911, at age nineteen.

I detoured off State Route 19 onto Cemetery Road a half hour ago after spotting this isolated cemetery on the top of a hill. My back is propped up against a small maple tree, and I'm trying to imagine who Arthur Haley was. The only clues are the dates of his birth and death. I wonder if people called him Art.

A gentle breeze is passing through the tree leaves, and a small airplane is flying overhead, but other than that it's quiet. It's only me and about two hundred people who lived in a time before mine. Cemeteries have a way of calming my nerves. They are quiet places, full of history if you look closely. When I visit a cemetery, my life gains perspective; one day I'll be in a place like this, and that's good to remember. The thought keeps me humble.

I had a brief talk a few minutes ago with a Mr. James Nixon, who died November 4, 1900, at age sixty-five. A NATIVE OF EN-GLAND, his grave marker read. I said hello to him and told him it was a warm and sunny morning, and that the grass on his grave was trimmed nicely. I only hoped he was paying attention, wherever he is these days.

Each grave has a story. In only a few words it sums up a person's lifetime. What the marker does not reveal, though, is the final ceremony at each grave when friends and family came to say good-bye. I sometimes try to imagine the scene. In 1911, when Arthur Haley died, friends and family probably arrived by horse and wagon. Dying at age nineteen, it's likely his parents survived him. Where I now sit, his mother may have wept on his father's shoulder.

William R. Wallace was buried in 1916 at age fifty-one. His family wrote a tribute and had it engraved on his granite marker:

> In memory of your dear
> Husband and loving papa.
> O, How sadly we do miss you.
> No one else but us can tell.
> But God who loved you better
> Has taken you home to dwell.
> You are gone but not forgotten
> And your memory shall never fade.
> And our lonely hearts will linger
> Where one we love so much is laid.

It isn't the best verse, but it's from the heart.

There are a lot of Dyers and Pentecosts buried in this cemetery. Lt. Elvin L. Pentecost, an army flier, was lost in flight during World War II at age twenty-two. His body is somewhere else, but a plaque commemorates his life.

Chester R. "Buzz" Dyer was buried in 1986. His wife of fifty-one years, Roberta, is still alive. Her place is reserved on their twin grave marker. The couple were married September 14, 1935. LOVE LIVES ON, the marker says. How lucky they were to have had each other so long.

Not far from the Dyers' marker is a small gravestone with a lamb statuette on top, a sure sign that a child is beneath. This grave belongs to Margarite L. Crane, who died in 1912 after living only thirty-four days. As you stand before this grave, you can imagine a young mother grieving here for her baby daughter. She and her husband wrote a poem:

We had a little treasure once
She was our joy and pride.
We loved her perhaps too well
For soon she slept and died.

And there is the marker of Jasper and Alice Livingston, both born in 1844. No date of death is noted, only the words, WE WILL MEET IN HEAVEN. Standing before their simple grave marker, I hoped they did.

I stop at many cemeteries in my travels. Some people think they are morbid places—to be avoided at all costs. These people, I suspect, are anxious about their own deaths, and a cemetery is a vivid reminder of a day to come. My feeling is a cemetery is a good place to celebrate life. Seeing the headstones and realizing that I am not under one is reason to cheer. It's like finding your name missing from the obituaries in the morning newspaper.

One of the most moving experiences I've ever had at a cemetery was the time I visited my recently departed grandmother, Anne Woodbury, at her grave in Grass Valley, California. It was two weeks before Christmas, and I had stopped to be with her for a few minutes during the holiday season. She had added such joy to so many of my Christmases that it was only right that I visit her for this one.

I had stood by her grave only a few moments when I heard faint sounds from nearby—Christmas music. Thirty yards away, I found the graves of Norma Lee and Geri Lee Jones. Norma died in 1980 at age forty, eleven years after her daughter Geri Lee died at age six. Now, near their graves, a small tree was strung with colorful bulbs. Cedar wreaths with big red ribbons rested against their headstones. In between, opened wide, was a white musical Christmas card playing "Joy to the World," "Jingle Bells," and "Rudolph the Red-Nosed Reindeer." The sound carried for fifty yards in every direction.

Modern technology—a microchip in a paper card—played music to two people in particular, and to hundreds of others in the process. I listened for ten minutes, all the while thinking about Norma Lee and Geri Lee: *Do you hear the music? How sad they died so young. Are you together now? I hope so. Is it the Christmas season where you are, Norma Lee and Geri Lee? Yes, I'll bet it is.*

Whoever brought the card believed so, too. He or she figured a mother and daughter would enjoy Christmas music no matter where they were.

You are lucky, Norma Lee and Geri Lee, that somebody loves you so much to think of you this way at Christmas.

The card played over and over, and it was as beautiful as a symphony. I left happy that Norma Lee and Geri Lee were not forgotten, and it was even nicer knowing that the Christmas music was drifting to my grandmother's resting place as well.

Tonight I'm in range of television. What a treat! It's Tuesday, and I have no idea what's on, but at least I can watch something. This will be my first TV in a week. In twenty minutes the local news will be on. I'm near the town of Bend, Oregon, so the local newscasters might be pretty entertaining all by themselves.

The decision I have to make now is should I watch the TV on my two-inch Watchman or on the big set? I think tonight I'll go first-class and watch the five-incher.

When you want to relax, sit by a campfire. I can't think of many things more comforting than a campfire. Whether alone or with friends, a campfire has a way of putting you at ease. Conversation by a campfire is relaxed. Life moves in slow motion, and problems go away.

Feeling the fire's warmth, seeing its orange glow, hearing its crackle, smelling its aroma, and watching its flames dance randomly into the air combine to make a campfire a simple delight.

The saying "the best things in life are free" is certainly true with a campfire.

Bugs are not making my day. I'm trying to write an article at a Forest Service picnic table, but bees are buzzing me, monster ants are attacking my leg, and an unbelievably big, hairy and ugly insect just landed between my T and Y keys. It has twin stingers dragging from its rear end—resembling the tail guns of a B-17.

But, worst of all, tiny "no-seeum" flies are trying to climb inside my computer through the sides of keys. I don't think the computer chips would appreciate such an intrusion.

Damn! Just as I was proofing what I've written so far, a "no-seeum" crawled inside my computer through a space by the cursor key. There's no way to get him out. He'll die in there, probably right on top of the most important computer chip. All I can do now is wait. I'll know if the fly does any harm because the computer will start throwing in strange letters, or turning words into somethkingg liiky2we thuw3b?lw tpin7wc wn 8ex!pm% + x>e

An *Out West* staff meeting has concluded here in the Bear Hollow Campground near Fossil. It was a fairly typical meeting— the whole staff showed up, which means one person, me. This is crummy for dialogue, but great for decisive votes. The staff voted to build a campfire as its first order of business. But it wasn't much of a campfire because the wood was rotten, so it burned too fast.

The meeting progressed well with no idle chatter. The only other camper in the park was not invited, primarily because he was a hundred yards away and that's a long way to walk when you don't feel like inviting somebody in the first place.

The second item of business was for the editor to try to get into his right brain—the creative part. To accomplish this, he threw rocks into a nearby stream—the purpose being to take his mind off pressing matters. Throwing the rocks turned out to be a pleasurable endeavor, causing a ten-minute delay in the meeting.

Rock supply exhausted, the staff returned to the picnic table and campfire to consider important issues. Such as:

• How many pages to publish next issue? No decision was reached.

• Why the cows that were roaming around yesterday didn't show up today.

• Where to go tomorrow—north or east? The decision was postponed until morning.

• What to cook for dinner after the meeting? Barbecued chicken was ruled out because it was still frozen.

• Why the name *Nikki* was carved deeply into the picnic table. Just who was this Nikki person and why did he or she carve up this particular picnic table? *Eric* also carved his name in the table. Why?

With no further business, the editor moved to adjourn the meeting. There was no argument, so he seconded his motion and the meeting was officially concluded.

It was a good staff meeting.

Like weird, wacky places? Pack your bags, stuff your pockets with nickels and dimes, and point your Chevy toward Lakeview, Oregon, along Highway 395. What you'll find is Jim Schmit's Lakeview Fantastic Museum, a five-thousand-square-foot collection of some of the weirdest stuff west of Winnemucca.

Among the items: President Eisenhower's inauguration Cadillac, a trailer once used by Elizabeth Taylor, a display of outhouses, two of Bing Crosby's fishing rods, miniature houses "built by a one-handed blind man," and a mummy named Olaf.

Most of the collection was displayed at the 1962 World's Fair in Seattle. Schmit bought it after its original owner died. He and other local citizens hauled everything to Lakeview in pickups, cattle trucks, and anything else with wheels. "The caravan was a mile long," Schmit recalled. "When we got home the whole town was waiting for us in the parking lot."

Lakeview (population three thousand) is the largest town in Lake County, an 8,359-square-mile expanse with only 7,600 residents (that many people live in only 1.2 square miles of Los Angeles). The area is so far from anything some people say it's "behind the sagebrush curtain."

The Lakeview Fantastic Museum has many music machines: nickelodeons, juke boxes (Al Jolson sings "Mammy" on one), an automatic violin, and even a mechanical hula dancer. And everywhere, toy people talk, sing, and dance. As visitors pass, controls under the carpet activate some of the machines, including a life-size laughing lady from an old boardwalk carnival.

Many of the games reflect their times. One offers NEW PROOF HITLER IS STILL ALIVE. Push a button and a curtain rises to reveal an imitation skull turning slowly on its neck while its eyeballs roll. An arcade game from the late 1940s lets players shoot an antiair-craft gun at Japanese soldiers.

A framed copy of an 1849 advertisement offers trips by AERIAL LOCOMOTIVE FROM NEW YORK TO THE CALIFORNIA GOLD FIELDS. The blimplike contraptions would supposedly make round-trips in a mere seven days for fifty dollars a person. "It may be anticipated that within a few months these aerial machines may be soaring in various directions at different elevations," the ad stated.

Perhaps the strangest exhibit is Olaf, a nine-foot, 650-year-old mummy born in about 1335 and found in Norway in 1888. Evidence suggests that Olaf was either a convicted criminal or a murder victim.

Too bad Olaf wasn't born in the 1960s. At nine feet tall, he'd be a cinch to be number-one pick in the NBA draft.

Small towns can be grouped into two categories—those that are doing well, and all the others. Those not doing so well figure there is a good way to improve things: attract tourists. The problem, of course, is figuring out exactly what will attract them. Pioneer museums aren't the way.

Wallowa County, Oregon, is a beautiful spot, but far from a metropolitan area—and far off the beaten path. It's in the northeastern part of the state, and not on the way to anywhere. The whole county has less than eight thousand residents, mostly in the towns of Enterprise and Joseph. In an attempt to lure some tourists, they invented a lake monster. Actually, they didn't invent the monster—they resurrected an Indian legend about a huge beast in Wallowa Lake that supposedly ate two Indians who were out for a canoe ride.

The few modern folks who say they've seen "Wally" claim he is a huge serpent—a cousin, perhaps, of the fabled Loch Ness Monster. Of course, most local folks figure if Wally is anything at all he's a log or big fish—a sturgeon, perhaps.

Whatever—it doesn't matter to the chamber of commerce,

which says there is a monster in the lake, and that's that. Scientific investigation is neither needed nor welcomed. What is welcomed are tourists.

The Monster Observation and Preservation Society has even been formed to hold a special BYOB&B (Bring Your Own Beverage and Binoculars) each year. Dozens of Wally fans show up to eat Monster Burgers and talk about their favorite lake serpent. Some of these folks scan the lake with their binoculars hoping to see Wally himself. So far, no luck. Wally is a good hider.

"Please join us at JC Penney for the Mr. Oregon Male America Pageant," read the ad in the Portland *Oregonian*. I reread it—yes it was for *Mr.* Oregon, not *Miss* Oregon. While I've never been a big fan of beauty contests, this ad struck a nerve. I had three initial reactions:

1. Who cares?
2. How stupid.
3. I couldn't win.

It was the third reaction that bothered me. My feeling was I wouldn't have a prayer of winning because I don't look like Robert Redford or Tom Selleck. My look is, shall we say, generic. According to the ad, contestants would be judged on the following:

HANDSOMENESS: Right there I'm dead. My muscles are in the two places I use most—my brain and behind, and my biceps are only slightly larger than my wrists. My waist is still slim, but not of award-winning dimensions.

POISE: I sometimes slump my shoulders when I stand, I slouch in a chair, and I say *warsh* instead of *wash*. So I'd fail this category.

PERSONALITY: I'd do OK here. When they asked me what I wanted to do with my life, I'd say I want to become a TV news anchor in a top-twenty market. When they asked me what I'd do if I won a lottery, I'd say I'd give the money to the poor and homeless. When they asked me to name my favorite Americans I'd say Ronald Reagan and Vanna White.

SWIMWEAR: In a hundred years, you would not get me on stage in my swim trunks. First, the only way to distinguish between my stomach and chest is that one is higher on my body, and the other has a belly button; they are, I believe, the same size.

Second, I have a truck-driver's suntan—a dark left arm and pale right one. Third, it's nobody's business how much hair I have on my chest.

FORMAL ATTIRE: To me, formal attire is a freshly washed pair of Levi's, so I'd fail this category.

Needless to say, I won't be entering this contest.

Rude people make me so angry. Most Americans are considerate, but the ones who aren't can make it miserable for the rest of us. I often notice this rudeness in campgrounds. I can't tell you how many times I've pulled into a peaceful campsite only to have someone pull in an hour later with the world's largest portable stereo. These folks, for some reason, want to share their music— usually rock and roll—with other campers, without ever asking them if they're interested, which they are not. They just turn up the volume, drink beer, throw hatchets at pine trees (I have seen this happen), and listen to what a lot of other people would have trouble considering music.

Walkman stereos, those very small units with headphones, are a great invention because they enable people to enjoy their music without disturbing others. Unfortunately, most rude people prefer to share their music rather than be courteous.

It frustrates me.

USA Today ran an article the other day about how we baby boomers are finally admitting we won't live forever. Most of us always expected we would.

The article explained how our bodies are changing. In typical *USA Today* fashion, the newspaper ran a fancy chart with arrows showing the parts of a typical middle-aged body that fail first— double chins, fatter midsections, thinner skin.

I looked in a mirror and, sure enough, the chart was right. Disgusting.

We can blame some of this physical change on gravity. Gravity is seldom mentioned at cocktail parties or on TV commercials, but it has a lot to do with some of our everyday complaints.

If you have achieved middle-age or greater, then you have perhaps complained of a beer belly or double chin, to name two possibilities. Both are caused, in part, by gravity.

Take me, for example. I weigh only ten pounds more than I did in high school, yet my waist is five inches wider. Gravity has done this to me. It has pressed me toward the ground with such force that it has transported some of my chest to my navel area. I have been wondering, in fact, if I could counteract this effect by sleeping upside down. What do you think?

Short people can complain about gravity with good reason. If it weren't around, their bones would grow without resistance, enabling them to grow taller. When we enter a true space age, when children are born and raised in zero gravity, they will be taller than their counterparts back on Earth. They will make good basketball players.

Gravity is good because it keeps your food on your plate, and forces water down the drain. But it is not all that it's cracked up to be. I thought I should bring this to your attention.

Chipmunks can wage war. I know that now. This afternoon, in an Oregon state park near Bend, a couple of chipmunks hit me up for some food. One stared at me and wagged its tail—just like a cat. Another one stood on his hind legs and sniffed.

So I broke down and fed them some Cheez-Its—a monumental mistake! The chipmunk grapevine works fast here, and in a few minutes there were a dozen chipmunks around me and more on the way. I fought to keep them from jumping on my lap, but it was a losing battle. Finally, I hid in the motor home.

About a half hour later, the coast clear, I went back outside to read. But within minutes the chipmunks were back in full force. I tried to ignore them but they wouldn't cooperate: "Cheez-Its, Mister, give us Cheez-Its."

I told them my Cheez-Its were gone. But they wouldn't listen. I told them they were bothering me. "Go away," I ordered. But they continued to demand Cheez-Its.

So I did next what any angered human would do: I declared war. I went to the motor home for my weapon. Outside, the enemy waited, some on their hind legs sniffing their button noses for the first wonderful whiff of crackers.

But they got no such treat. I returned with a fully loaded spray water bottle, adjusted to shoot a straight stream of tap water with each squeeze of the handle.

A chipmunk warrior near Bend, Oregon

So the rodents who sought Cheez-Its got water instead—right in their cute little faces. To my surprise, they did not surrender. Soon, wet chipmunks were attacking—veterans of an earlier assault. The thought struck me that *they were enjoying this war*! One made at least eight trips, each time reaching within a few inches of my shoes. "Shoot me, I dare you!" he barked. So I shot him. He would shake his head when hit, make a squeak, then retreat to the woods. Out of my range, he would roll in the dirt and prepare for his next attack. "I will get the human's Cheez-Its," he mumbled under his breath. And then he charged again. Some were masochistic—coming very close to me then taking two or three blasts of water before retreating. These were the kamikaze chipmunks.

As I fought bravely to keep these aggressive minibeasts away, I noticed a boy of about eight in the distance. He was running through the woods with a green "machine gun" squirt-gun—raging his own battle with the chipmunks. This campground was under siege! Then the terrible thought hit me: *The chipmunks were winning!*

As I considered possible defeat, I recalled another chipmunk encounter near Lassen National Park. I was inside the motor home writing at my kitchen table. The front door was wide open. Suddenly there was a noise. I looked up and a chipmunk was standing on its hind legs checking me out. I knew what he wanted.

But before I could even move, he had raced across the floor and leapt onto my lap. He stood on his hind legs and stared at me with huge brown eyes. "Mister, I want Cheez-Its. You give 'em to me now, and there won't be any trouble, OK?"

Well, I wasn't going for it, so I shook my leg, sending him flying into the air. He landed softly on the carpet, only his pride injured, and he darted out the door.

But my present battle wasn't ending so easily. In fact, it showed no sign of even ending at all. Finally, after twenty minutes of fighting, my ammunition and confidence were running low. Rather than prolong my inevitable defeat and waste ounces of precious Pacific Northwest water in the process, I retreated to the motor home, a defeated man.

The rodents shook hands and celebrated.

*   *   *

CHUCK WOODBURY

Outside the porta-home's back window, in the Spokane River, the trout are jumping like crazy. It appears that the creatures are in need of a meal. Unfortunately, I am in Washington, and my fishing license limits my fishing to California, so I will not be able to catch any of these tasty creatures for my frying pan.

This is how the sport of fishing works with me: When I am in California, where I can legally fish, the fish are never hungry and thus never bite. When I am in other states, the fish are always starving, and will bite anything that moves.

But there is more to this story. If, tomorrow, I were to buy a one-day Washington fishing license, the fish would find out. They would not jump as they do this evening, nor would they have any appetite at all for my hook, even if it were smothered in the finest fish bait money could buy.

I am an unlucky fisherman, and, to be honest, a lousy one too.

We humans are lucky: We don't have to worry about a predator gobbling us up in a single bite. Other creatures do.

A few minutes ago, I was sitting on a rock on the shore of the Spokane River, taking in the gorgeous scenery and savoring the cool air. A few feet in front of me, in six inches of water, an inch-long trout swam by. Twenty feet away, in deeper water, its bigger cousins were enjoying an evening meal of flies and bugs. Later, their tastes might turn to something more aquatic—like the little fish that just swam by.

"You'll be lucky to make it to your first birthday," I advised the baby trout, but of course it didn't hear me. As far as its simple little brain could understand, life was nothing more than an endless swim in the shallow water. Just wait until it meets its first two-pound lunker.

Mosquitoes. I hate the little blood-suckers. For five minutes I've been stalking one around the porta-home. My weapon is a rolled-up K Mart newspaper insert, the perfect weapon for creatures smaller than one ounce.

The creature landed on my seminaked, half-awake body earlier with one purpose in mind: to stick his needle-nosed, tubular-shaped blood-sucking mechanism into my unsuspecting, nutrient-rich flesh. The microvampire is in for a surprise, though, because it

146

made the fatal mistake of flying first past my ear—buzzing as it went.

Ooh-ga, ooh-ga, a warning horn sounded inside my head. It sounded like the "dive" horn on a WWII submarine, and it alerted me that the micro blood-eater was out for a fast snack—in the form of *my delicious red blood*!!!

"My, my," said I, "the fly must die."

And so now, armed with my twelve-page K Mart newspaper insert, I am stalking the good-for-nothing minipunk.

The object of my search has apparently decided to take a spin around my porta-home, perhaps to work up an appetite for dinner. It has no clue that it is doomed—to be swatted into virtual nothingness by a hand-powered, twelve-page, full-color newspaper insert.

As I prepare to stalk the bitsy beast, I am getting angrier and angrier. The gall of this nearly microscopic creature to even think of eating me—even a part of me. No bug sucks my blood and lives to brag about it.

I will stay up all night if necessary to find this pint-size vampire. It will die as surely as the sun will shine tomorrow (I heard the forecast earlier on Channel 8, so I know).

I am seriously on the prowl now—checking the ceiling, the imitation-paneling walls, the refrigerator door, the door to the porta-toilet. *No bug.* I am searching the lights. *No bug.* I have just shaken a window curtain. *No bug.* Has the creature escaped through a crack in the insulation? Hopefully not.

Madder and madder I grow by the moment. But with each passing second I am storing up extra energy in my right arm. It will be called upon soon to propel the K Mart newspaper insert toward the bug. The arm will be responsible for wiping the miniature menace from the face of the motor home and the Earth itself.

Now, as I hunt, my mind thinks about this creature, the mosquito. What a huge meal a human body must be. I cannot imagine what it must be like to be face-to-face with a potential meal at least fifty thousand times your size. To a human, it would be the equivalent of a cheeseburger the size of the Houston Astrodome.

But back to the matter at hand—killing the pest. I vow that my porta-motel is one porta-motel where this mosquito will check in, but not out.

Ten minutes have passed. No bug.

Five minutes more have passed. No bug.

12:10 A.M.: *positive bug sighting.*

Flying erratic pattern from back left window to center of ceiling. Two o'clock high at present. Totally unaware that it will expire within moments. Still under impression its meal is in upper bunk, sleeping.

The bug has landed. One small step for bug, one giant step for mankind.

I am ready. The K Mart insert is folded tightly in my hand. I raise my arm back, angling it perfectly, getting ready to swing. *Curtains for the bug is imminent.* I pull my arm forward with unbelievable thrust—like an F-15 on take-off. Then . . .

"No!" I shout. How can it be?

I have missed the bug! *Tell me it isn't so!*

But luck is with me. The pea-brained insect has flown to a wall and landed again. The creature has bought an additional thirty seconds of life. *Big deal!*

Again, I grip the K Mart insert—even tighter than before. In my head I am chanting: *Kill the bug, kill the bug.* I am psyched. *It's time.*

I cock my arm. Again I follow through with a powerful swing. Then there is a tremendous *pla-thud* sound. The K Mart newspaper insert has hit the wall. With luck, the bug will be in between.

Or is it?

I pull the paper away slowly to inspect the wall. I look carefully. What do I see?

There is no bug on that wall!

"Noooooooooo!" I scream.

Is it possible that I missed? Was my swat that far off or that powerless? At my age have I lost my ability to kill? Have I gone from being a young, virile bug killer to a weak wimp who can't even waste a crummy bug? *No. That can't be true.*

So I check the K Mart insert, holding my breath, hoping to find the you-know-what. And then (drum roll) my heart skips one beat—two beats—three beats and then *four whole beats*! Am I happy or am I dead? I cannot tell. Four beats is a lot of beats to miss. Irregular heartbeats can kill you. I know that from the doctor on *Eyewitness News.*

But I pinch myself. Yes, I am alive. *Alive!* It's great to be alive and be a citizen of the greatest country in the world (Canada is nearly as good, but too cold in winter).

Do you know why I am so happy? Because right on that K Mart insert—right on top of the picture of the purple bath towels, right next to the picture of the blue sheets is the following: one bug, dead as a dinosaur.

It's time for celebration—Miller Time. But all I have is a yellow can of generic beer. BEER, it says in 48-point Futura Bold.

It will do.

I'm a happy man.

It's 10:00 P.M., and I'm in a campground that was peaceful until twenty minutes ago. That was when the couple in the trailer up the road drove away. They left their dog behind, and it hasn't stopped barking. And it is a loud, obnoxious bark.

This happens a lot, so I spend a lot of time figuring out a solution to this annoying problem. And after many hours of deep thought, I arrived at one: Tranquilizer Milk Bones.

It's very simple—feed dog biscuits laced with Valium to a barking dog. It will fall asleep almost instantly. No mess, no beating—no more barking.

This idea has merit. I hope some company picks up on it.

A blue mood has me in its grasp. Part of my depression is because the motor home isn't running well—it started running roughly a couple of days ago. And I'm not in the mood to stop for a day while a mechanic I don't know tries to decide how much money he can make from a tourist in trouble.

And another crummy thing about today is that tomorrow I have to drive into downtown Seattle for a 9:00 A.M. appointment. The thought of driving the RV in city traffic terrifies me. I have visions of missing an off-ramp and ending up in Portland, or mowing down one of those urban motorcyclists who delight in racing between the lanes.

So, here I am in La Conner, Washington, parked in a municipal parking lot, making a grilled-cheese sandwich to drown my misery. I've already burned one side of the sandwich, and I still have another side to go. It's that kind of a day.

Actually, I shouldn't even be here. I should be sightseeing on a ferry boat in the San Juan Islands. Unfortunately I had a little problem earlier. I drove all the way to Anacortes to catch an early-morning ferry. I parked in a dirt parking lot where buses shuttle foot-passengers a few miles to the docks. After I'd waited a half hour, a bus showed up, loaded up a dozen of us, and headed off.

About five minutes later I had a terrible thought: *I forgot to lock the motor home!* I recalled a news article about some crooks who had been ripping off ferry passengers' vehicles lately. *They'll get my two computers, two printers, and two cameras!*

I worried all the way to the docks and was still worrying when we arrived and everybody got out. Everybody except me. "Please take me back," I told the driver.

In a half hour we were back at the parking lot. The motor home, of course, was locked.

Talk about being mad.

Cities smell. When you've been in the country for a while, you really smell the city when you drive through. I just drove through Seattle. The minute I got near town, I could smell it—mostly the exhaust from automobiles. After smelling pure country air for a couple of weeks, it smelled terrible.

Driving south on I-5, the same smell was in Tacoma and even in Olympia. South of Olympia, the air cleared and became sweet, interrupted only occasionally by the smell of cows at a dairy. Even though I don't care much for the smell of cows, it's better than the smell of car exhaust.

Yesterday I read an article in the *Daily Astorian* that said: "Americans looking for a pristine wilderness experience on remote U.S. Forest Service lands increasingly are finding trashy campsites, unsafe trails, unhealthy water, and pollution." At the time, I concluded that my experiences had been good, especially regarding campsites. Most have been very clean.

Then I checked into Silverlake State Park, across Washington State Route 504 from the Mount St. Helens Visitors' Center. My campsite is gorgeous, except for one thing: The camper who was here before me must have cleaned some fish, then thrown the heads into the bushes. The place stinks. I suppose the person who left the fish heads is the same one who throws Burger King wrappers from his car window. I have no respect for this kind of person.

The man in the trailer down the road is playing a clarinet. He plays a scale or two, then a simple song, then another scale, and so on. He and his wife live in Ontario, Canada, and are touring the states with a twelve-foot travel trailer. At this very moment, both he and his wife are inside the trailer. I can hear his clarinet from about thirty yards away. His wife, also inside the tiny trailer, must be going crazy.

The guy is no Benny Goodman.

It occurred to me today that people in campgrounds act a lot like they do at home: They keep to themselves. In our very urban world, people often don't know their next-door neighbors. We no longer need them for anything. In the old days, when grocery stores were few and far between, it was nice to have a neighbor around to lend us some sugar or butter. Now, we just walk to the corner 7-Eleven store—no need to bother the guy next door.

It is much the same in campgrounds. People pull into their space and stay to themselves. RVers can hole up inside their rigs without ever going outside—as they often do. Other campers stay around their own campfires, with little interest in what's happening a few yards away. They don't know their next-door neighbor at home, so why should they know their next-door camper? Older people still seem more interested in their fellow campers, probably because they are of a generation when knowing those near you was important.

The return-address labels on some of the letters I receive include the wife's name before the husband's. Instead of John and Jane Smith, it will be Jane and John Smith. Is this a new trend?

One place, though, where tradition is still intact, is inside the automobile. You seldom see a woman driving with a man riding shotgun; 99 percent of the time, the guy drives and the woman rides. It's the same on a motorcycle and tandem bicycle—the guy is up front, the woman behind.

In campgrounds, you find further evidence of traditional roles. The men putter around outside, while the women cook dinner and

151

attend to the kids inside the RV. The man will cook only when the meal is being prepared on an outdoor grill. Tradition dictates that women cook and men barbecue.

But a lot more women are mowing lawns. Ten years ago you seldom saw a woman mowing a lawn. It was a man's work. Nowadays, a lot of women are raising a family alone, or living alone, and they have to mow the lawn or else live in a field of weeds.

Of course, some of these female lawn mowers may be sharing chores with their husbands. If you could peek into their kitchens, perhaps you'd see some guys washing dishes.

Another thing I've noticed—and I hope you don't think me too strange for bringing it up—is that it is impossible to look a person in both eyes at once. I don't know what made me think of this because there is nobody around to even double-check this with. But I know from experience with girlfriends that you can only look into one eye, then into the other—but not both eyes at once! You can fake it by looking at the top of a person's nose. To them it will appear you are looking into both their eyes. Of course, this is unsatisfying to the looker because all you see is a nose, which is not very appealing.

Give this a try. It's pretty interesting.

There is some very weird stuff at Marsh's Free Museum in Long Beach, Washington, including a half-man, half-alligator named Jake. Admission is free, but 90 percent of what's inside is souvenir shop rather than museum. Still, the 10 percent part is terrific.

Take Jake the Alligator Man, for example. He's displayed in a glass case on top of an old music machine. The creature looks like a mummified dwarf, except that from the waist down he's alligator and from the waist up he's man. Some people believe Jake is made of plaster; others claim he's real.

"I don't think it's real, but nobody can figure it out," a store employee explained to three Japanese girls who were gawking at the weird creature. Personally, I thought Jake looked a little phony; I wish I could have slipped a hand under the glass case to cop a feel.

But Jake is only one attraction at the sixty-seven-year-old museum. The two-headed calf and two-headed pig are pretty neat; so is the eight-legged lamb. All are very dead and stuffed, of course.

There are many old music machines, each with a brief historical note. "I played for more than fifty years in a Bawdy House in LaCrosse, Wisconsin," a message on one explained. Another machine plays "He's a Good Man to Have Around" on a violin and piano. The piano part is OK, but the violin sounds awful.

I couldn't resist an old nickle machine that I thought showed a silent movie. It was titled *Nudist Colony*, which got my attention. So I checked around to be sure nobody was watching me as I made my "movie" selection. The coast clear, I dropped in a coin, placed my eyes in the viewing scope, and eagerly awaited a 1920s version of *Debbie Does Dallas*. Instead, a light came on, revealing a few tiny, nude ceramic figures—as sexy as Betsy-Wetsy dolls. Disappointed, and five cents poorer, I resumed my tour of Marsh's.

There were snakeskins nailed to the ceiling, and all sorts of collections on the walls—handguns, saw blades, even some old hand fans—one with a color painting of Franklin D. Roosevelt on one side. A shrunken head from the Jivaro Indian Jungle in South America is popular. Museum visitors spend a lot of time staring at this fellow who, besides being old, is quite dehydrated and ugly.

At Marsh's Free Museum you can see a melon plug ("used to see if a melon was ripe"), a vampire-bat skeleton, a shell from a 665-pound turtle, and a foot-warmer used on sleigh rides. Museum owner David Wellington said he keeps adding to the collection.

If you want to take something home, you can purchase a clam shell for ten cents, a Jake the Alligator Man T-shirt for $8.50, a Jake bumper sticker for fifty cents, or a stuffed blowfish for twenty-five dollars (my favorite). When you've finished exploring the museum you can walk across the street to the small amusement park (complete with bumper cars and shooting gallery) and to a park featuring the world's largest frying pan.

When I was a child, my biggest fear was that an alligator was lurking under my bed. No matter how much my mother reassured me, I knew there was an alligator—or perhaps something far worse—only inches away, waiting to tear me to pieces with razor-sharp teeth.

For much of my childhood, I was preoccupied with this fear. So I spent a lot of time hiding under my blankets—a convenient fortress. Alligators or other monsters, I reasoned, could not attack people hidden by blankets. It was a good tactic, for I was never attacked by an alligator in all those years.

Today, I am convinced that there are no monsters under my bed. Now they are outside my motor home, and like the alligators, they come at night.

They come mostly when I am alone in a remote campground. These monsters are not reptiles, but bad men—very bad drug-crazed men who will kick in my door and shoot me with hollow-pointed bullets, then rob my limp, lifeless body of all its cash.

On a dark night, far from another human being, I can have this irrational fear, especially when a howling wind makes many strange and eerie sounds. The fear is worst when a car appears in my dark campground at 3:00 A.M. Why is it there? Who is inside? Who would come here at such an hour? Until the car leaves, it's alligators under the bed all over again.

Even though I am a grown-up man, and well aware that evil men rarely lurk in campgrounds, I still worry. You can call me a wimp if you wish. I guess what makes this fear as bad as the one of my childhood is that nowadays I know that hiding under my blankets is a lousy defense.

I don't know what I'm going to do when my fish flashlight quits working. My niece got it for me for Christmas. It's about the size of a four-inch bass, and when you squeeze its gills, light shoots out of its mouth. It's the best flashlight I've ever owned. The only problem is you can't put in new batteries when the old ones die. That's a shame, because there is nothing much you can do with a four-inch plastic fish.

A sign on Morse Street reveals a lot about Ryderwood, Washington: RYDERWOOD, NOT JUST MORE YEARS TO OUR LIVES BUT MORE LIFE TO OUR YEARS. Ryderwood is a town for folks fifty-five years and older; most of its 350 residents are over sixty-five.

It looks like many other small towns in the Pacific Northwest with its modest wood homes along tree-lined streets. Newspapers in the 1950s called it "The first successful retirement community in America." Originally a logging town, Ryderwood was converted into a retirement community in 1953 by businessman Harry Kem.

"People here live on their Social Security—that's what we do," resident Jewel Santineau told me. Actually, Kem planned it that way in 1953, selling only to elderly couples with permanent incomes of $125 to $250 a month.

The town is at the end of State Route 506, fifty-six miles north of Portland. "You hardly ever see a car coming up the street," says Santineau. "If you see two in a row, that's traffic." Santineau and her husband moved to Ryderwood in 1986, paying twenty-two thousand dollars for their three-bedroom home. Nowadays, she plays drums at local dances and is a member of the town's motorcycle club, the Gray Angels.

The Ryderwood Cafe is town headquarters. Residents show up each morning to exchange information, dine on owner Edith Grant's pancakes, and celebrate birthdays and other special occasions. By tradition, the person doing the celebrating furnishes the cake and pays for everybody's coffee.

Ryderwood is so peaceful that deer often feed on apples in residents' trees. Sometimes at night, the howl of a coyote can be heard from the nearby forest.

One of the most interesting things about Ryderwood is the volunteer fire department. The average age of the brigade is seventy years. No young whippersnappers accepted, for sure.

It's a rainy day and the earthworms have risen. They are all over sidewalks and in the gutters of streets, seeking sanctuary from their flooded subterranean world. Many have already been crushed by automobiles, bicyclists, and mailmen. These worms, less intelligent than even a cow, are unaware of their predicament. Instinctively, they wiggle their way onward at a pace slower than a slug's, seeking a soft spot where they can dig their narrow bodies downward. For many, it is a death crawl.

Some will be crushed, some will drown in the puddle from a sudden downpour, others will be eaten by robins, and many of those still alive will turn to worm jerky when the sun reappears. A few lucky ones will survive to eat dirt again.

Be thankful you are not a worm.

A black cat, looking very sad and hungry, was sitting on the cold, damp ground behind my motor home when I awoke this morning. So I fed him two slices of lunch meat. He gulped it down like he was starving.

I spent about fifteen minutes at my picnic table talking to the wild feline, which would not let me nearer than ten feet. I told him how pretty he (or she) was, and that he could trust me. But he didn't do anything except let out an occasional sad whine.

I felt sorry for the little fellow, and wished I could have packed him up and taken him along. But he would never let me catch him, so there was no need to even consider that thought. Still, I hated leaving him there in the cold forest.

The trouble with a cat is that once it makes up its mind to be wild, it will be that way forever. A cat is not smart enough to figure that a guy like me who feeds it good food means no harm. Of course, I cannot fathom what it is like to be wild. I have always been tame.

Cats are lucky in one respect: They are covered with fur. The reason I say they are lucky is that with so much fur, they age better. The fur hides their wrinkles. We humans have no fur to hide our wrinkles. Clothes help, but we don't wear clothing on our faces, which get wrinkled from sun exposure.

Cavemen and cavewomen had lots of hair. We look at these primitive old-timers and say, "How ugly," or "How disgusting." Perhaps we should be kinder. Perhaps, in fact, we should consider that in a million years, because of the disappearing ozone layer, humans may become even hairier than those Stone Agers.

Without today's ozone layer to protect future beings from the sun's evil rays, many will die before they reproduce. Their hairy friends, protected somewhat from the evil rays, will live longer and will thus reproduce in greater numbers. Each generation will thus become hairier. After thousands of years, these hairy beings will take over.

So the next time you see a drawing of a caveperson, consider that you may be peeking into the future.

Speaking of furry creatures, I have long felt that if you want to become a millionaire, there is one invention that begs to be invented. Whoever invents it will make millions of dollars. What I am speaking about, of course, is a cat that never has to go potty. I refer to this animal as the "crapless cat." Personally, I will be the first in line to buy one.

The makers of cat litter, I'm sure, would not be eager to see such an animal invented. But with such amazing progress in genetic engineering these days, they should at least consider the possibility.

Technology continues its progress in the newsrooms of newspapers. I called a reporter at the *Los Angeles Times* today. A machine answered, then instructed me to enter the extension of the reporter by pushing the appropriate buttons on my phone—which I did. After two rings, the recorded voice of the reporter answered: "I'm not at my phone right now, but if you leave a message at the tone, I'll return your call."

Tally on the call: two machines, zero humans.

I was just thinking about some goldfish I once owned. I wondered what they would have thought of me if they had a bigger brain? How would they explain me? What would I be to them?

Surely, I thought, I could be nothing less than a god. For I fed them, purified their water, and protected them from evil. That, it seemed, was enough to qualify me as a god.

What could they think of my world if they had brains? Could they ever imagine such a place existed? Could they conceive of a huge ball of dirt and water twenty-five thousand miles around and thousands of miles deep? Could they conceive of billions of fish? Could they conceive of a forty-ton whale? Could they even conceive of another fishbowl somewhere?

"Do you suppose there are other worlds besides ours?" one might ask the other. "Do you think that our god has created only us?" They would stare from their bowl for evidence, but would see none.

If I were those goldfish, I could not envision another one-gallon fishbowl anywhere, much less a world twenty-five thousand miles around. Many times, as I observed my fish, I wondered about my own god and the world he created for me. Am I in his fishbowl? Does he bring me food and change my water? Does he, or another god, have other worlds that I cannot even imagine? Is my god as real yet as unexplainable to me as I was to my goldfish? Smart goldfish could only wonder. Just like me.

CHAPTER SIX

NEVADA, NEW MEXICO

Manhattan, Nevada, is a ghost town that barely hangs on to life. I met one of its hundred or so residents, Dennis Johnny Locke, outside the Manhattan Club, the local watering hole and gathering place. He was giving tax advice to another fellow.

"I'm not an accountant, but I help people with their taxes around tax time," he said. "I'm a photographer." Johnny, it turned out, spent about two decades in the radio business, working at stations in the San Francisco bay area, Sacramento, and Reno. In his mid-forties he got burned out, and ended up moving into a trailer house in Manhattan. But there's phone and mail service, so Johnny earns his living taking photos for business cards, calendars, and portraits. He told me about all his photo equipment and it put my modest setup to shame.

It's amazing the talented people you find in some tiny, out-

159

of-the-way places where you only expect to find prospectors or hermits.

There's a little dried-up mouse at one end of the Manhattan Club. He's got a piece of wire in his mouth. The story goes that the little critter got to chewing on an electrical cord, and he bit into it a little too deeply and got electrocuted in the process. So, years later, his last moment is preserved atop an upside-down cup at the Manhattan Bar. The rodent didn't know he'd become so famous when he bit into that wire.

Don't look for the town of Carver's on your map. Chances are, it won't be there. It's a bend in State Route 376, about midway from Tonopah to Austin. It's one of three settlements in the huge Smoky Valley, home to the world's largest heap leach gold mine.

The Smoky Valley is a huge treeless expanse of dirt and sage-brush with thousands of sagebrush for every human. Highway 376 is a mostly straight two-laner with 180-degree views of high-rising mountains to the sides, clear air above, and a lone procession of telephone poles ahead. It's as remote a place as you'll likely find in the contiguous United States. Until a few months ago, residents north beyond Carver's used generators for their electricity.

Carver's is in the innards of Nevada, surrounded on all sides by wide-open spaces and outposts that are either ghosts, semi-ghosts, or candidates for ghosts. Nevada towns have a history of boom and bust—based on the gold supply of their local mines. Goldfield, Austin, Eureka, and Manhattan are a few such towns, each rich in history and heartbreak.

About eighteen hundred people live in the area—mostly min-ers and their families. Round Mountain, with a few shops and post office, is the big settlement, but a couple miles away is Hadley, a brand-new company town for present Round Mountain residents whose land is too rich in gold to remain unmined. Carver's is six miles up the highway toward Austin.

Carver's and its neighboring settlements are enjoying a boom, now that local mines spew out gold like McDonald's does burgers. Spend some time around here, listen to a few conversations, and you'll get an idea of what life was like in the Old West.

The hot spot in Carver's is a transformed truck stop called

Carver's Country run by Sue and Greg Scott. It's a local hangout with video store, pint-size casino (fifteen slot machines, one blackjack table), restaurant, Laundromat, and car wash. Video rentals, by the way, are big business; the nearest movie theater is 235 miles away.

Greg was busy selling gas and renting videotapes when I stopped by, so Sue did the talking. She said Greg had always dreamed of turning something in the middle of nowhere into a successful business. She'd gone along with his dream, and seems satisfied with the results.

"I've never cared much for city life," she said. "I've always been a country hick. I'm happy here." Today, she divides her time among work, home, and two-year-old daughter, Melissa, the reigning "Little Miss Royalty of Nevada."

At work, she sometimes deals blackjack, but mostly she supervises the Carver's Country staff of thirty-five full- and part-time workers. Though things are pretty comfortable today, "there were times when we should have given up," she said.

Nowadays, miners stop by to eat, gamble or play pool, rent a

Greg and Sue Scott, Carver's, Nevada

video, or buy gas. Tourists sometimes ask to see Rene Zavil, who has been cooking at Carver's Country since 1948. Except for the time she broke her arm, she's never missed a day of work.

Something I've learned recently is what rural westerners would like to have in their towns that they don't already have. They would like a K Mart. I suppose if you live in the middle of nowhere with only a general store, a huge discount place like K Mart would be real welcome.

Urban kids probably don't appreciate what it would be like to live far away from their school. Sandee Guglielmo of Round Mountain told me about her son who attends high school in Tonopah. He leaves home at 6:30 A.M. for the ninety-minute bus ride to school. He plays sports, so he stays after regular classes. A special bus for the athletes brings him home to Round Mountain at 8:30 P.M., which gives him ten hours to sleep and get ready for the next day's trip.

Something is fishy about the stories I get from operators of historic hotels. It seems that Teddy Roosevelt spent the night at about two thirds of the old hotels in America.

On about every tour of an old hotel, the guide or manager will come to a certain room, open the door, and say, "Teddy Roosevelt slept in this very room," or "Teddy Roosevelt spoke off this balcony." Now maybe sometimes it's true. But I think in other cases, they are repeating a tale that originated years earlier. Either that, or Teddy did a lot of sleeping around.

Butch Cassidy also got around, except he robbed banks. Everywhere you go in the West it seems Butch was there before you. There's even a plaque on a building in Winnemucca that says Butch Cassidy and his gang robbed the place when it was a bank. Historians say Butch never set a foot in town, much less robbed a bank there. But don't tell the people of Winnemucca that.

When your pet passes on, you might want to take him or her to Carson City where the pet cemetery is operated by the city and county of Carson.

People bring their animals from great distances. One man hired a hearse to bring his dead dog 450 miles from Los Angeles. A woman from San Francisco has come three times to bury her pet turtles, bringing each in a handmade redwood casket.

"They aren't big turtles," animal-control director Michael Conklin told me, holding his hands three inches apart to illustrate. "They're those little green ones."

Carson City opened the cemetery in 1980 to help offset the costs of animal control. It's the only pet cemetery Conklin knows of that's run by a municipality. "At first, I thought this place was a crazy idea, but now I think it's something that should be done in other communities. People know that because the cemetery is municipally owned it won't get bulldozed over in five years for a subdivision."

Headstones bear names like Tipper Reynolds, Propwash Hoke, and Shagnasty Poindexter. Most of the graves contain dogs and cats—more dogs than cats. But there are some parakeets, a snake, the three San Francisco turtles, and a horse.

"We had a tough time with the horse," explained Conklin. "We did our best to bury it in a professional manner. It was difficult using the backhoe to get it into the grave." But he said it was good experience: The animal's owner has two more horses coming sooner or later.

Inside the building there's a small reception room where grieving families make funeral arrangements. Some customers purchase a preneed plan, before Rover or Tabby actually expire. A local minister often performs graveside services. There's usually a viewing ceremony first.

Conklin figures the cemetery won't fill up for another six or seven years, unless, of course, customers bring in a bunch of horses.

Jackpot, Nevada, is a dry and dusty splotch of civilization in the desert along the Idaho border. It's loved by jackrabbits, Idaho gamblers, and tired motorists heading north or south on U.S. Highway 93—which, with the Pan American highway to the south and the Alcan to the north, forms the longest route on the continent.

I first visited Jackpot twenty years ago. Back then, marquees on two casinos advertised the same entertainer. She would apparently do a show at one place, then walk across the street to perform at the other.

Nowadays, Jackpot has grown up. There's an airport, golf course, and several big casinos. Right next to Cactus Pete's is the Jackpot National Forest—about a half acre of pine trees. It's a joke, of course, but an appreciated one in this expanse of desert. The streets of Jackpot are named Ace, Casino, Twenty-One, Dice, Keno, Roulette, and Slot. So while Jackpot may not have much vegetation, it at least has some humor.

Jackpot has the smallest overlap time zone in the United States—three quarters of a mile long and a quarter-mile wide. Although the settlement is in the Pacific Time Zone, Mountain Standard Time is observed as a convenience to the gamblers who arrive mostly from Idaho.

Last night in bed, my mind was racing so fast I couldn't sleep. Story ideas kept popping into my head. Just when one would get over with, another one would pop in. At times like this, I write the thought in a notebook, then rip out the page and throw it from my upstairs bunk to the floor. Some mornings, I awaken with a dozen pieces of paper scattered about. Usually about three ideas are good. The other ones are stupid. It's amazing how a half-asleep mind can think an idea is good when it actually stinks.

Last night I was ripping paper out of that notebook like crazy. About midnight I looked to my floor. The brown rug was gone—buried by pieces of paper. But I wanted to sleep. So, to take my mind off story ideas, I tried to remember which team was leading each division of the NBA. All I could come up with was the Lakers. Then, I put on my Walkman stereo. I went through tapes by James Taylor, the Beatles, and Roy Rogers. Then I read a few pages from Mark Twain's book *Roughing It*.

The last thing I remember was looking at my clock at 2:00 A.M. Six hours later, I stepped down from my bunk onto a sea of notebook paper. It was a good night for ideas, but a lousy one for sleep.

*   *   *

164

Tonight it's cold and windy outside, but the air is clean and there's no traffic noise. My computer is up and running, my stomach is full of a motor-home–cooked meal, and my bed is ready when I am.

Tomorrow I'll head down a road I've never traveled before, and that is very exciting. I have no idea what I'll find. Maybe I'll find a bunch of stories or make a friend. But maybe I'll meet nobody and find nothing of interest. It's like fishing: You put in your line and see what happens. Sometimes you get a trout; sometimes you get a carp; sometimes you get skunked.

It's not knowing what you'll get that's fun. I love being a nomad.

For the last four hours, I've been writing while parked outside the Riverside Resort Casino in Laughlin. My little generator produces just enough power to run my computer, printer, and a few lights. It's a wonderful feeling, sitting here in the parking lot with a personal power plant cranking out electricity.

The other day, while driving over Hoover Dam, I realized I had something in common with that huge slab of concrete. We both generate electricity. I admit that the five hundred watts my Honda generator produces is far less than what Hoover Dam can generate with its huge turbines. Still, it's a powerful feeling to know that I'm sort of a little Hoover Dam all by myself.

Laughlin is an amazing town. Twenty years ago, it was a dusty spot of desert with one tiny bar run by a guy named Don Laughlin. Today, there are nine gambling casinos and nearly five thousand hotel rooms. Laughlin is twenty-five miles north of Needles, California, on the Colorado River across from Bullhead City, Arizona. It's a boomtown that's growing like asparagus.

One of the best things to do in Laughlin is ride the ferry boats from one casino to another. They zip up and down the Colorado River like fighter planes in a combat zone. The casinos line the river, so you get off wherever you want. There's no charge.

The casinos allow RVers to camp for free in their parking lots and the result is an eyeful of aluminum and an earful of portable generators. Some campers stay for weeks.

The Laughlin crowd is older than the one in Reno, Las Vegas, or Lake Tahoe—about ten years on average I'd guess. Most of the action is at slot and draw-poker machines. Gamblers are relative low rollers compared with their counterparts in Las Vegas.

There are more cheap buffets here than anywhere else in America. You can stuff yourself for four dollars or less for dinner— even less for breakfast or lunch. Generally, when I visit Laughlin I can expect two things: to lose money and gain weight.

A while back the town of Pahrump billed itself as "the Palm Springs of Nevada." What a joke!

Pahrump is about an hour's drive from Las Vegas. It has two golf courses, one that's very nice and is the basis for the comparison with Palm Springs, which has about a hundred courses.

Downtown Pahrump, if you can find it, has a few cafes, a gambling casino/hotel, gas stations, a bunch of real estate offices and some mom-and-pop businesses, including a hardware store with GOD BLESS AMERICA painted on its side.

Dining out is presumably popular, but you can leave your formal attire at home. A few dining hot spots are Betty's Feedbag, Big Olaf of Pahrump, Cotton Pickin' Restaurant, Dough Boy Bakery, and the No Name Cafe.

The town setting is pretty, with mountains all around, including Charleston Peak and the Spring Mountain range to the east. Pahrump is an Indian word meaning "water on a flat rock."

In its early years, the Pahrump Valley was an important camping spot for explorers, traders, and Paiute Indians. Later it was known for its wine, brandies, and cotton. Now, notes chamber of commerce literature, the valley is known for "an exciting new fall crop of lettuce."

If you find lettuce crops exciting, Pahrump is your kind of place.

I was driving from Death Valley to Beatty along lonely Nevada Route 374, which has no airwatch airplanes and never will, when all of a sudden there was a huge bone-dry lake bed out there in the middle of the Amargosa Desert. It was so big you could land a Boeing 747, stop, and then take off without turning around.

There was a little road leading on to the lake bed, so I decided to take it. Of course, there was an idea in the back of my head that would make this side trip an especially good one. *The idea had to do with the golf clubs packed away in my closet.*

Well, I drove out on that huge sunbaked lake bed, doing a couple circles and figure-eights on the way, but eventually parked dead-center in that huge expanse. I then bundled up in a sweater and jacket, for it was very cold and windy, grabbed a number-three wood, two orange golf balls and one yellow tee, and walked a couple dozen yards to a place that looked right for the number-one tee.

Of course, there was no yardage marker, so I made one up: "1,327 yards. Par 9." I then planted the tee in between a crack in the hard-packed dirt, placed the ball upon the tee, and began to look over the course, taking some practice strokes at the same time.

Then, satisfied that everything was right, I proceeded to take a gigantic swing with the intention of sending that particular orange golf ball halfway to the Burro Inn in Beatty.

But instead, the ball rolled twenty yards and stopped.

Undaunted, I fetched the orange orb and returned to the yellow tee, mounting the ball and vowing this time to send it into the ozone. I carefully took my stance, pulled that number-three wood forward so smoothly and nicely you would have thought it was Arnold Palmer at the tee. And then my club met the ball so perfectly it made a *swoosh* sound the likes of which that dry lake bed had never heard before.

And it can be told here and now that the orange golf ball took off so high it nearly achieved orbit over that dry lake bed in the Amargosa Desert. It flew so high it looked like an orange UFO as it sped toward Highway 95 and Beatty beyond. It was up there with the geese and the Cessna 172s and the high-flying bugs.

There was no slice, no hook—just a ball on a direct flight southeast. It was up there so long that I went back to the motor home, made a tunafish sandwich on wheat, ate it, then returned to the golf course to see the ball land 925 yards away.

The second ball went the same way.

Well, I then fetched the balls and hit them again and again, following a triangular course over that dry lake bed, playing a perfect game, making par all the time, hitting that ball so beautifully it was a shame ESPN wasn't there to televise it to golf fans in Missoula, Tuba City, and West Covina.

During the entire game, not another golfer showed up to play, and only a couple of cars passed on the distant highway, and they were unaware that a one-person golf tournament was being played right there on that dry lake bed in the Amargosa Desert.

It was sport at its best.

There's a Carl's Jr. ad in today's *Las Vegas Review Journal*. It advertises a Country Fried Steak Sandwich: "Discover an old-fashioned American value right out of the country," the ad says.

I don't understand. What is so *old-fashioned* and *country* about a fried sandwich at a Carl's Jr.? At the bottom of the ad, it says, "We Still Believe in Old-fashioned American Values."

I wonder what old-fashioned American values they're talking about. I've eaten at perhaps twenty Carl's Jr. restaurants and do not recall seeing, feeling, hearing, or otherwise experiencing anything resembling "Old-fashioned American Values."

To be fair to Carl's Jr., I have not found old-fashioned American values at McDonald's, Burger King, Taco Bell, or at any of the other one billion franchised food places in America.

Carl's Jr. should change its ad to: "At Carl's Jr., we promise, like every other franchised food place in America, to give you fairly good food, fairly fast, on a clean table where you can eat it, and we'll furnish clean restrooms which you may need now that they're not in gas stations anymore."

That would be a better ad.

The word "homemade" is abused in many restaurants. "Homemade" pies are advertised, but they are really "restaurant-made." The restaurant should advertise them as "Pies made on the premises." If they really are made at somebody's home, then they could legitimately be called *homemade*.

Today on the radio, I chuckled at the message on one ad: "We're not in the mall, so there's no mall overhead." I didn't catch the name of the store because the radio signal was weak, but this was the first time I'd heard an advertiser claiming an advantage by not being located in the mall. Usually, being at the mall is a plus.

The rule of advertising that applies here is this: Size up your pluses and minuses, and if you don't have any pluses, make one up.

Car dealers use this rule all the time. The big-city dealer says he can save you money because he "deals in volume." The guy in the little town says he can save you money because of "low country overhead." Which one is telling the truth?

Nowadays, it's fashionable to advertise how friendly and help-ful your employees are. Commercials show employees with big smiles, running across the sales floor to help you. When's the last time an employee treated you this way?

This is hardly the time to bring up something about Christ-mas, but as I was writing about good, old-fashioned values earlier I remembered some notes I made to myself last Christmas. They were about Santa Claus. I wondered: "Do we ever see a Santa Claus these days who isn't selling something?" It seems to me that Santa Claus is selling more products than even Ed McMahon. For example, in department stores and malls he's selling photos. Your kid waits in line to see Santa, and then when he gets on his lap, they pose for a photo. The hope is you will buy some prints. On TV, Santa is selling about anything and everything. Isn't it ridic-ulous to see Santa riding on a Norelco electric shaver each year?

Two weeks before last Christmas, Santa walked through the restaurant where I was dining, passing out coupons for a free yo-gurt cone and five dollars off a haircut. Is this the same fellow who climbed down my chimney in 1953 with a brand new Marx electric train?

Seeing Santa pitch one product after another disturbs the child in me.

I was strolling on a sidewalk in Hawthorne this morning and was startled by the sound of an auto horn a few yards away. I looked toward the noise and saw a fox terrier up against a steering wheel pressing on the horn. I was preparing to snap a photo, when the dog's owner rushed out from a nearby store. "Now stop that, Pepe," she yelled. I asked her if Pepe honked the horn often and she said he did.

Some dogs bark. Pepe honks.

Now that we can legally drive sixty-five miles per hour again on some highways, motorists are routinely going seventy to seventy-five. When the limit was fifty-five, people drove sixty to sixty-five. There is an unwritten rule in many motorists' minds that says the speed limit is the speed posted, plus five to ten miles per hour more. If you drive the speed limit anywhere—freeway, city street, or country road—you will have a dozen cars on your bumper in no time.

Most Americans are law-abiding citizens, but when some of them get on the road, they turn into outlaws.

Yesterday, I passed up two opportunities of a lifetime. That's what two radio ads said in Socorro, New Mexico. "Videos are only eighty-nine cents a day Monday through Thursday," one announcer said. "Don't miss this opportunity of a lifetime."

A few minutes later, a guy was selling artificial cigarettes. You smoke these things, then supposedly lose your desire for regular cigarettes. The announcer said his deal was "the opportunity of a lifetime." So, in one day, in one town in New Mexico, I passed up two opportunities of a lifetime. Too bad for me.

I must have pulled over for twenty cars and trucks yesterday. It wasn't that I was going too slowly—I was traveling the speed limit most of the time. It's just that the motorists behind me wanted to go faster. So I pulled over, even though it was inconvenient most of the time. Of those twenty I let by, only two thanked me: A trucker blinked his lights and a guy in a car waved.

Eighteen drivers went on their way, not taking one bit of effort to raise their hands to say thanks—even though I went out of my way to be considerate to them. When they do that, I wish I could turn back the clock twenty seconds, and then let them wait there behind me.

My motor home is a home in motion. The wind is really howling outside, the windows are flapping, and the floor is swaying; if I didn't know better, I'd think I were in a huge earthquake. I'm camped in Roswell, and the gusts of wind are whipping dust all around. The problem is that it's 80 degrees outside, so if I keep my windows shut, the motor home turns into a sauna bath. If I open the windows, dust comes flying in. For now, I've got the windows shut, and I'm stripped down to my shorts.

Right now I'd prefer to be in a Motel 6—or any other place that doesn't shake, rattle, and roll. I'm facing possible seasickness if the wind doesn't calm down soon.

The problem with wind is it wears you down. I can't explain exactly why, it just does. Someone suggested to me the other day that many rural people look weathered because of all the wind they put up with. Personally, I think the sun has more to do with it. Still, by the end of a windy day, I'm pooped. I go to sleep, but wake up the next morning still tired. After a few days of this, I'm in no mood to do anything but go somewhere without wind.

What's so great about staying at a fancy hotel or motel that charges you $150 a night? I have stayed in these places, and take my word for it, they are not so hot. They are so clean they are boring. Sure, you can order room service, and there's a phone by the toilet, and in the afternoon a maid drops by to put a chunk of chocolate on your sheets. Big deal! I'll take a cheap room with a phone by the bed, and I'll buy twenty bags of M & M's and pocket the hundred bucks I save. Let's not forget the purpose of a motel: to sleep. Who cares if the wallpaper's peeling when you're out cold?

Give me a place with a Magic Fingers. Give me a place with a cheap painting bolted to the wall. Give me a place with a three-speed air conditioner. Give me a home where the buffalo roam.

I hate room service anyway. I'd rather put on my shoes and walk to Denny's.

The biggest difference between being on the road and being home is the wind. At home, a wind storm is no big deal. Your home doesn't rock with every gust. On the road in a porta-home, the wind is significant. When you are driving, it can send you into another lane—which is not healthy if an eighteen-wheeler happens to be heading your way. When you are camped, it can cause you to shake, rattle, and roll when you would prefer not to.

Rain, cold, and hot temperatures—even a light snow—are easier to deal with than a severe wind.

I bought a gallon of generic drinking water today at Safeway. The label on the plastic bottle read: DRINKING WATER, PREPARED BY REVERSE OSMOSIS.

171

I didn't know what reverse osmosis means, so I went to my *Webster's New World Dictionary*. Here's what it said: "A method of extracting essentially pure, fresh water from polluted or salt water by forcing the water under pressure against a semipermeable membrane, which passes the pure water molecules and filters out salts and other dissolved impurities."

To me, that sounds like it's filtered water. That's how Safeway should have labeled their water: PREPARED BY FILTERING. People understand the word *filter*. I'd buy the water if it said that.

You hear people say they'd like to have lived in a simpler time—like a hundred years ago. They're tired of polluted air, traffic jams, high taxes, stressful jobs—and all the other problems of the 1980s.

I know what these people mean, but they might think about some of the drawbacks to returning to those simpler times. Like what if they needed a tooth pulled? There were no pain killers except maybe a swig of whiskey. What if they had a headache? No aspirin.

Women took a big chance when they had a baby; complications killed many of those mothers. And the babies very often didn't make it to their first birthdays. A lot of parents in the old West buried a lot of their children.

The reason I was thinking about this was that tonight while building a campfire I got a tiny splinter in my finger. I tried to pull it out, but failed, so I tried to bite it out but that didn't work either. I finally had to go into the motor home for tweezers.

Those people who want to go back in time probably never considered what life would be like without tweezers. Long ago, folks probably walked around with a bunch of splinters in their hands.

Today I bought four newspapers. When you are a newspaper-aholic, as I am, you buy whatever local newspaper is on the newsstand. I was surprised to find four newspapers at the local Town and Country Food Store here in Roswell. So I bought the *Roswell Daily Record, Lubbock Advance-Journal, El Paso Times*, and *Albuquerque Journal*. All the papers had pretty much the same national news, which you'd expect.

Three of the newspapers had an ad from Radio Shack. I recalled that most of the newspapers I buy have Radio Shack ads—even tiny weekly papers. Radio Shacks are about everywhere, even in small towns. They are terrific stores because they have many nifty electronic gadgets. I've bought battery testers, walkie-talkie and short-wave radios, mini black-and-white televisions, battery chargers, and even a remote-control dog—my favorite purchase.

The dog operates like a miniature race car, moving forward or backward on electronic command. Cats are petrified when you send it in their direction. A dog I know named Max goes raving mad when he sees the remote-control dog in action. He wants to tear the bloody thing to shreds.

Get yourself a remote-control dog if you have a chance to. They make great pets, except when their batteries go dead.

The Cattle Baron Restaurant in Roswell offers dishes like catfish ($6.95), New York steak ($10.95), and chicken teriyaki ($5.95). It thus surprised me to find a $16.95 peanut butter sandwich on the menu.

"Made from authentic Gouber Gulch peanuts grown in the renowned Portales Valley," it explained. The Portales Valley, I learned, is famous for its peanuts. But *$16.95*?

"It costs $19.95 if you want jelly," said my waitress Ava.

It's all for fun, of course, but apparently a few people have ordered it.

I should stay around Roswell for a few days. The reason is that on Sunday they are having a "Cow Plop" at a local school. The Roswell television station was running a public service ad for it yesterday.

You're probably wondering what a "Cow Plop" is. It's a fundraiser in which contestants purchase a small painted (or drawn) circle on a field. Then, when all the circles are sponsored, a cow is let loose. You win if the cow plops in your circle.

I walked into Manny's Buckhorn Tavern in San Antonio with a hungry belly and a stuffed-up nose. After one Buckhorn Burger, my stomach was full and my nose clear. A Buckhorn Burger is a half pound of New Mexico beef covered with cheese, and smothered with a glob of fresh green chile that goes down like fire; it's better than Vicks for clearing out a nasal passage.

Manuel "Manny" Olguin, sixty-nine, and his fiancée, Anita Casaus, serve about thirty-five hundred Buckhorn Burgers a month. They personally shape each patty and peel and roast the locally grown green chiles. A Buckhorn Burger goes for three dollars.

Sunday is the busiest day at the Buckhorn, when tourists show up in swarms to down about two hundred to three hundred burgers. Manny and Anita each work twelve hours a day, seven days a week, swapping chores as bartender, cook, waiter—and in Manny's case—guitar, accordian, and piano player.

The Buckhorn Tavern is in downtown San Antonio a half mile from the Rio Grande. The restaurant is a rustic place with wooden floors and chairs, and deer heads and sombreros on the wall. The bar has six stools and a carved eagle in its midsection. Manny opened the Buckhorn in 1949, and for years it was a popular pool-playing and drinking spot for the local good ol' boys. Nowadays, the pool tables are gone and the drinkin' toned way down. Mostly tourists show up now to eat a Buckhorn Burger.

"A lot of people learn about the burgers at the airport in El

Manny Olguin and Anita Casaus, Manny's Buckhorn Tavern, San Antonio, New Mexico

Paso or Albuquerque," said Manny. "We get tourists here from all over the world." Fifteen years ago, Anita was one of those tourists. "I ran out of gas at one in the morning, so I knocked on Manny's door to see if he could pump me some," she recalled. In 1983, she came back to San Antonio to retire. She began dropping by the Buckhorn for some companionship. "When two people are living alone and are lonely, they just find each other," she said.

The Buckhorn isn't the only place in town with famous hamburgers. The Owl, up the street, is also known for its burgers.

No McDonald's, though.

Met a fellow today in his mid-sixties. "Got a girlfriend from Germany," he told me. "She's fifty but has a body of a thirty-five-year-old." He flashed a devilish grin. "Want to see her picture?" Curious, I nodded. So he grabbed his wallet, fiddled around a bit, then held up a color photo—of a woman wearing no clothes. "She's proud of her body," he said to wide-eyed me as he passed the photo to another equally wide-eyed guy nearby.

I wonder if she knows he's flashing her picture.

Have you ever driven a hundred miles hoping to find something and then when you got there discovered it wasn't there?

That happened to me.

I had spotted a little hollow dot on my New Mexico map while driving U.S. Highway 60 near Show Low, Arizona. "Pie Town," it said. It was the smallest dot on the map, which meant there were probably from zero to five hundred people there.

But with a name like Pie Town, you figure there must be a cafe named "Mom's Pies," or something similar. You figure you might also find a souvenir shop that sells T-shirts and hats printed I ATE PIE IN PIE TOWN.

That's what you expect from a place called Pie Town.

But do you know what? You can't even buy a single piece of pie in Pie Town—not even one of those Hostess hand jobs that comes sealed airtight in wax paper. Do you believe that?

About the only locally made things you can buy in Pie Town are home-grown tomatoes. Talk about disappointment!

You can buy some things at the High Country store which, with its dirty concrete-block walls and concrete floor, looks more like a car garage. Other than the tomato place, the High Country store is the only business in town.

Cal and Olean Williams run the business, selling gasoline, potato chips, cigarettes, peanut butter, infant formula, toilet tissue, soft drinks—things like that. But they do not sell pies. "Oh, I've thought about it," said Olean. It turns out that a cafe up the road sold pies. But the owner was hurt in an automobile accident so the restaurant is now closed.

Pie Town got its name from cowboys who once drove their cattle through the area. They'd stop to eat some homemade pies, so they started calling the town "Pie Town." Tourists and truckers also stopped for pies, until the Interstate went in up north and traffic through town slowed down. The cowboys quit coming in about 1970.

Today, sixty-five people live in Pie Town. Only a few have regular jobs. "They're a pretty independent bunch," said Cal Williams.

The Williamses moved to Pie Town a year ago from Idaho. He's got a bad heart, and the brutal winters in his old home town weren't doing him any good. Even though Pie Town is on the Continental Divide at eight thousand feet, Cal likes the climate.

"People say there's no oxygen up here," he said. "But just look around—there's trees for a hundred miles. And what do you think gives off oxygen? Trees."

He and Olean live next door to their store in a four-bedroom house with four dogs—three part-wolf and a pocket-size half-Chihuahua named Little Bit.

Cal's doctor in Idaho told him to limit his exercise to walking. Work was out of the question. But Cal didn't go for that, so even though he's got a mechanical heart valve clicking inside his chest, he still works six days a week. He said he doesn't sleep very soundly, which is OK because many nights someone knocks at his door after midnight wanting gas. There's no other gas station for twenty-two miles in either direction on U.S. 60.

They don't earn much off their tiny business. "We're turning into a pawn shop, even though we don't want to," said Olean. "People down on their luck trade us something for gas. We buy and sell some piñon nuts, too."

Olean has been thinking about the name of the town, and that

Cal and Olean Williams, Pie Town, New Mexico

perhaps she should capitalize on it. She isn't about to start cooking pies, but she's got another idea. "I'd like to find somebody who makes printed mugs," she said. "I think if I printed some up that said Pie Town on the side, that people would buy a mug with their coffee."

She asked what I thought of the idea. I said it was good and that I'd probably buy a couple of mugs. I told her if I had to leave Pie Town empty-tummyed, at least I wouldn't have to leave empty-handed.

Melissa Rucker does her talking in sign language. Her vocabulary is two words: *Stop* and *Slow*. Rucker, thirty-five, is a flagger.

A few years back, she would have been called a flagman, but that's sexist. You could call her a flagwoman, but flagger is a better word. She was working on two-lane U.S. 60 between Pie Town and Quemado, when she ordered me to halt.

She had been there three weeks, out in the middle of nowhere, only her and miles of sagebrush, and a few guys up ahead riding on some machines widening the road. During the summer, Rucker works as a fire lookout.

Melissa Rucker, flagger on U.S. 60, near Pie Town, New Mexico

"This is more boring than being on the lookout," she told me. "You can't read." So what does she do, out there alone on the road all day? "I ponder," she said.

There are three certain things in life: birth, death, and a Gideon Bible in every motel room in America. When you check into a motel or hotel, you will always find this Bible in a drawer. There will also be three envelopes with the name of the motel, three pieces of letterhead, and a ballpoint pen.

Hotel and motel owners are not necessarily religious people. It's just that the people who make Gideon Bibles send them free to every motel they know of. Motel operators figure the Bibles are free, so why not put them in their rooms? It's a good deal for everybody.

But what I'm wondering is this: Are the folks who distribute the Bibles concerned that a lot of people nowadays stay in RV parks instead of motels? It would be a huge marketing problem, figuring how to get a Gideon Bible into the drawer of an RV. It's a lot easier to get one into a room at Motel 6.

Wow, do I have something to tell you! It's about the underground restaurant in Carlsbad Caverns. In the Underground Lunchroom, the sun never shines.

The eatery is 750 feet below the earth's surface inside New Mexico's mammoth Carlsbad Caverns. To get to it, you can walk for a couple of miles along a steep trail, or ride an elevator and arrive in sixty seconds. Either way, a ham and cheese sandwich is ninety-five cents.

When you dine in the Underground Lunchroom, the rest of the world could explode and you'd never know it. It's like being on another planet. The rock ceilings are low, the lighting subdued, and the climate odd-feeling. If you're like me, you might expect some Morlocks to show—remember them from H. G. Wells's *Time Machine*? The lunchroom temperature, like the rest of the caverns, is 56 degrees whether you dine in winter or summer.

Customers order food cafeteria-style, and young folks in matching shirts serve the grub. Food fare is limited to cold sandwiches, snacks, beverages, and box lunches. There are even restrooms—flushers. These are no "Johnny on the Spots"—they're

"Johnny in the Caves." A pump transports everything back to the surface for disposal.

A phone booth is available for visitors who want to call some-one back on Earth, and there's even a mini post office. MAIL A POSTCARD HOME, a sign says. Right next to the mailbox and post-age stamp machine is a rubber stamp you can apply to your post-cards: MAILED 750 feet underground, it inks. All kinds of things are for sale: T-shirts, postcards, Milky Way bars, View Masters, vid-eos, even hair combs that are stamped CARLSBAD CAVERNS.

Until the first lunchroom was built in 1928, cavern visitors had to bring their own food. Now you need only bring money, but not very much, because the food is cheap. Diners who aren't satisfied with the limited menu in the Underground Lunchroom can eat above in the main lunchroom, where a more complete menu is offered. But dining there is boring.

I overheard a little boy who showed up while I was dining underground. As he entered the cavernous eatery, he turned to his mother, and with eyes as wide as wide can be shouted, "Wow, Mom, picnic tables in a cave!"

When is a child no longer a child? I have wondered this for a long time, but I now have the answer: A child is no longer a child when he or she will no longer do a somersault. A six-year-old will gladly do a somersault. Ask an eleven-year-old, and maybe the child will do it. I asked my twelve-year-old niece to do a somer-sault. "It'll mess up my hair," she replied. With that answer, she was no longer a child—in my book, anyway.

Here's something you may have done as a child but have never talked about as an adult. I'm referring to playing doctor. Some of you played this game. I know so because years ago when my psychology professor brought up the subject, everybody gig-gled. You could tell it was because they all had done it.

I remember one particular time I played doctor. I had con-vinced a certain neighbor girl to let me inject her with a pretend shot. After an objection or two, she obeyed.

Little did she realize that young Doctor Chuck had obtained a real pin, which he intended to use as his instrument of healing. Of course, the naive doctor did not realize what pain such an "injection" would cause his unsuspecting patient. Little, too, did he imagine how loud his patient could scream. It was also unfortunate that the young doctor's mother was visiting with the patient's mother in a room only yards away.

So when the patient screamed, the wide-eyed doctor guessed correctly that it would not fall on deaf ears. He knew he was in for a heap of trouble. No longer caring to be a doctor, he fled as fast as his little feet would carry him to his house, locking doors behind and slipping underneath his bed to hide from certain punishment.

His mother, a few steps behind, was understandably upset at finding herself locked out. So she pounded on the door, ordering her son to let her in. The words *or else* came up often, as in "Let me in *or else.*" The young doctor, of course, didn't budge.

But, unknown to the young man, he hadn't secured at least one window. His mother thus gained entry and soon discovered his secret hiding place. Punishment was ultimately delivered by the young doctor's father upon his return from work. It was effective, for the young man never played doctor again. It was so effective, in fact, that from that day on, the youngster never had any desire whatsoever to be a doctor or even to visit one.

White City is the settlement right at the entrance to Carlsbad National Park—the only civilization for miles around. But as towns go, White City isn't much—a motel, restaurant, bar, souvenir shop, RV park, and The Million Dollar Museum.

Depending upon which tourist literature you read, there are either thirty thousand or fifty thousand items inside. Admission is $2.50, which figures out to either .0008 cents or .0005 cents per item, which makes visiting the place seem like a bargain. But after seeing it, I'm not so sure. I didn't find anything too interesting.

The dead bodies were OK; there are about a half dozen (plus some skulls), including two baby mummies. One's an infant less than a foot long, and the other is about a one-year-old. One adult is mostly a skeleton. "Apparently, the wild javelina had gotten to him as sections of the rib cage are eaten away," said a sign. My ribs ached at the thought. People who like mummies and skeletons may like this museum.

There are lots of guns, farm things, old typewriters, old violins, arrowheads, branding irons, fifty-three-gear clocks, and a few old cars, including a 1905 Schacht Roadster. I'd never heard of a Schacht Roadster, so I didn't get excited. To me, the car at "The Thing!" museum in Arizona that supposedly transported Hitler was more interesting.

Other items that didn't excite me included a 1976 Lard Press and Sausage Stuffer, a peanut sheller, the first letter boxes from the Roswell Post Office, and the miniature "Old West Cattle Drive." I didn't like the last display because you had to put in fifty cents to see it work, and I had already paid $2.50 and was not about to give Mr. White, or whoever owns White City, any more money.

I was also very disappointed in the two-headed rattlesnake. Four kids caught it in 1970. Nowadays, the reptile is shriveled up to about the size of a night-crawler worm. It didn't scare me a bit.

One good thing was the old Zenith TV with a perfectly round screen. But even better was a big old white bathtub. I'm not sure if I believe the message on its display card, but if it's correct, then this is a very good bathtub. The card reads: 17TH CENTURY BATH-TUB USED BY NAPOLEON. If that's true, then it's the most historic bathtub I've ever seen—maybe worth the $2.50 admission price all by itself. But probably not.

While on the road, I see mostly unfamiliar faces. Today, for example, I saw an older fellow with very wrinkled skin, yet he was wearing a blond hairpiece that looked right for a twenty-five-year-old. He was a strange, sorry sight.

But there is always one familiar face—the one that always shows up in my mirror. No matter where I am, if I look into a mirror, he'll be there. Just this morning, in an Alamogordo rest-room, I looked into a mirror and guess who was there? That's right, the same guy who was in the mirror the day before in White City.

Every time I look in the mirror, he's looking at me. I look away, but when I look back, he's still staring at me. The other day I told him to get lost. I told him I was sick of his face, and in the future I'd prefer to look at somebody different for a change. But he just looked at me.

I was so upset that I complained to the fellow who was washing up at the sink next to mine. He said he had the same problem, only it was a different guy. I asked him if I could look at his guy, and he said sure. So I peeked over into his mirror.

Do you know what I saw? The guy in his mirror was none other than the very same guy who was in my mirror. What in the world is going on here?

Sometimes in bed, an image will pop into my head of somewhere I have been on my travels. It may be a street intersection, a building, or the view from a campsite where I once spent the night. Most of the time I can recall the location, but other times I can't. So I will toss and turn for a half hour trying to remember. It's frustrating—the same frustration you feel when you can't remember the answer to a trivia question: "What was the name of Sky King's airplane?" would be an example. If, in your mind, you can visualize the plane, but not its name, then you will go semicrazy. This is the feeling I have when I can't identify a location that pops into my mind at night.

Sky's plane, by the way, was the Songbird.

In a regular home, you never worry that your bedroom is going to roll off a cliff. It's something you never think about—that is unless you travel in a motor home. Quite often, when I'm about ready to fall asleep, a terrifying thought forces my eyes to pop open and my heart to palpitate. *I forgot to set the parking brake!*

If I didn't set the brake, I know that I'll be dead by morning— a victim of a driverless, out-of-control motor home, rolling over a three-hundred-foot cliff at three in the morning taking its sleeping driver to an untimely death. It would be an awful way to die. So every time I get this thought I have no choice as to what to do: I climb down from my bed, walk to the cab, and check the brake.

Nine times out of ten, it's set.

CHAPTER SEVEN

UTAH

THIS morning, I stopped four times for cows on the road and to check out a coyote someone had killed and then hung up on a barbed-wire fence for the buzzards.

I drove 110 miles of Nevada Route 233 and Utah Route 30, and all together I counted fewer than thirty cars and two homemade billboards. Once, I stopped in the middle of the highway for ten minutes to take a photo. Another time, I backed up for half a mile. In Sacramento, I pass thirty cars in two seconds on the freeway; I couldn't stop five seconds without getting hit or honked at.

Today, the air was crisp and pure. I gulped it. Do urbanites even know this world exists? I know people who pay thousands of dollars to jet to some distant place on the globe for rest and relaxation. Do they know that this is so close, and that the price of a ticket is only a few tanks of gas?

This morning on the radio, the announcer was talking about a community event coming up in Wells, Nevada. It had to do with shearing sheep. I didn't get all the details, but it sounded like it was popular. It wasn't the kind of event you'd find in a big city.

Mack's Pharmacy in Brigham City is the place to go for fifteen-cent birthday cards. Mack has been in business for forty years at the corner of First Street South and Main. You get the feeling some of his stock was there the year he opened. "I used to stock up on inventory for tax purposes," said Mack. "Some of those cards are what you might call slow sellers."

Downtown Brigham City doesn't look too healthy these days. The old JC Penney store has moved away, as have many other stores. But they didn't move to the mall—that's not the reason. "It's demographics," said Mack. "All you find in the houses around here are old people. I remember times when there'd be thirty boys reading comic books on my magazine rack. They'd read for a while, then buy one for ten cents. I don't even stock baby powder anymore because there's no demand for it."

Mack's Pharmacy hasn't changed much through the years. Right inside the front door is the sign WILLARD TREATMENT FOR STOMACH DISTRESS. AUTHORIZED DEALER. Next to that is a penny scale that tells your fortune. I dropped in a coin. "You gain by being deliberate and cautious," it said.

I worry about things breaking down. When I am on the road, I worry most about the engine in my motor home quitting. Of course I also worry about my cameras, the photo enlarger, my computer—and the motor home's shower, water pump, and other mechanical conveniences.

A hundred years ago people didn't worry much about things breaking down—except for maybe their horse getting sick or their gun jamming before a shoot-out. They didn't worry about their stereo, television, VCR, or microwave falling apart. And lucky for them, they never had to do battle with a Monkey Ward salesman trying to sell them an extended warranty on a color TV.

Speaking of things breaking down, in retirement-oriented Sun City, Arizona, a prostate operation is so common among male residents that it's referred to as a "Sun City Tonsillectomy."

*   *   *

I've been studying the names of a few of the cities here in Utah. A fellow I met today speculated about the name of the town of Levan, which is smack-dab in the center of the state. "Spelled backward, it spells navel," he said. It turns out that Brigham Young named the town, and some folks believe he named it for that very reason. I guess Brigham Young had a sense of humor.

Centerville, you might think, would be in the center of the state. But no, it's between Salt Lake City and Ogden. The other day I stopped for lunch in Snowville, and I thought it was an odd name for a place not even in the mountains. Why Snowville? I checked around and discovered the town was named for a Mormon president, Lorenzo Snow. Farr West also interested me. I figured it must be on the western edge of the state, and whoever named it added an extra R to be different. But, no, that wasn't right. Farr West, north of Salt Lake City, got its name from pioneers Lorin Farr and Chauncey West.

Finally, you might think a town like Orangevale would be the center of an orange-growing region. Not so. The town was named after an early settler, Orange Seely.

One interesting town name I must check out, however, is not in Utah but in Washington. Its name is George. I assume it was named after the president, but you never know.

When is the last time you smelled dirt? If you are a farmer, you smell dirt. If you are a gardener, you smell dirt. But if you are like me, you seldom smell dirt.

As a boy, I smelled a lot of dirt. I drove my toy trucks over dirt roads I built in vacant lots. I played in dirt for hours, then took some of it home on my jeans.

Today, driving through the town of Cornish, a crosswind delivered the smell of dirt from a freshly plowed field. It was a wonderful smell. Almost in an instant, I recalled being a little boy building tiny dirt roads. I was down on my knees, pushing my toy truck along a six-inch-wide highway I had built in a vacant field. Smelling dirt was a good smell then, and it is a good smell today.

There are few things better than being a young boy and playing with toy trucks. Of my all-time best experiences, playing in the dirt with toy trucks is in the top ten. There was something magical about building imaginary roads, then guiding your vehicle along those tiny pathways. What makes this sort of thing so wonderful is our ability as children to imagine. A young boy with his toy trucks is a real truck driver; a young girl dresses up and for a while she is a lady.

The ability to imagine is so common in children, yet so uncommon in adults. As children we *dream;* as adults we *do.* Adults see things for what they are; children look at something and imagine what it could be.

To adults, the leaves are a mess, an empty cardboard box is trash, and a puddle is an inconvenience. But to children, raked leaves mark the rooms of a house when arranged in a certain pattern; a discarded box is a dark cave; and a water puddle becomes a lake for a paper boat.

Two young boys from the campsite next door are playing in the dirt outside my window, passing time before their dad takes them fishing. There is dirt on their pants and dirt on their faces, and probably dirt in places that do not show. But that's all right, because they are camping, and it's OK to get dirty when you are camping.

A little boy is happy by the campfire, along a trail, in a row-boat, atop a big rock, in a sleeping bag under the stars, or in a "fort" beneath a manzanita bush. A little boy can fish for hours beside his dad, and if he catches a six-incher he will talk about it for years. A little boy will delight in helping his father put up a tent, or in holding his stringer of trout. He will walk by his father along the shore of a lake as proud as any human being can be.

Camping is the best of all possible worlds for a little boy.

One thing I remember from my childhood is reading Superman comics before I went to bed. The idea was to fill my brain with Superman thoughts. There was a good chance that if I was successful, I would be Superman in my dreams.

So many nights I would fly over Metropolis, capturing villains and saving fair maidens. Lois Lane was never in my dreams, but I suspect some of my favorite girls from school were.

I have not dreamed of being Superman for a quarter century.

Nowadays, I dream of writing an embarrassing headline, or forgetting to include something important in an article.

Dreaming of being a superhero was much better.

Joe and Marie Caruso spend their days inside a big rock right along Highway 89 on the south side of Orderville, Utah. JOE'S INTERNATIONAL ROCK & GEM SHOP, it says on the sign out front, and right behind that is the craziest-looking building you've ever seen. It looks like a big rock, but it's really made of fiberglass and plaster. It's painted light pink, which blends in with the mountains all around.

The Carusos sell big rocks and little rocks and all sorts of gems to rock hounds and other visitors who drive and bus in from all over the planet. Joe owns a mine up the road where he and his two boys mine for septarium nodules—rocks with beautiful insides. Joe or Marie will sell you one for a buck or for $280, depending upon size and appearance.

This is the only place in the world with such septarium nodules, so rock collectors come from all over to check out the merchandise. They buy the rock by the piece or pound.

The Carusos sell Picasso stone, petrified wood clocks, and fossils. You can pick up a forty-thousand-year-old herring fossil for $3.50, which works out to only .00007 cents per year, not a bad deal. They also sell tiny plastic dinosaurs that glow in the dark ($1.25).

Besides selling rocks retail and wholesale, Joe has invented a machine that turns regular rocks into rock eggs. You throw raw rocks into a machine, and every few seconds it'll spit one out shaped like an egg. Joe and Marie then polish them up, slap on a price tag, and that's that. "Engineers say it can't be done, but I did it," said Joe.

The Zion First National Bank building at 3 West Main Street in Vernal is the only building in the United States that was delivered by the United States Postal Service.

When the Bank of Vernal outgrew its headquarters in 1916, a new building was planned—to be faced with eighty thousand textured bricks. They would cost only seven cents each, but freight charges to haul them the 175 miles from Salt Lake City would be four times that. Someone came up with an idea to mail them Parcel Post. A fifty-pound package could be mailed for half the freight charge. So the Bank of Vernal sent in the order, and forty tons of bricks were individually wrapped and put into fifty-pound bundles, the maximum allowed by Parcel Post.

Instead of traveling 175 miles directly to Vernal, they had to go 407 miles by standard gauge railroad to Mack, Colorado, then by narrow gauge railroad to Watson, Utah, where the railroad ended. The final 65 miles to Vernal was by horse-drawn wagon over rough roads and by ferry over the Green River.

Because the wagon journey took four days each way, mountains of Parcel Post bricks piled up at Mack, Colorado. The frantic postmaster telegraphed Washington for help; postal regulations were immediately changed to limit the total weight of any Parcel Post shipment to two hundred pounds in any one day. But it was too late, for the last bricks were already en route to Vernal. Eventually, they were all delivered and became part of "the building that was shipped by mail."

Vernal is a terrific town because it has all kinds of dinosaur things. Dinosaur National Monument is nearby, so the town has adopted a dinosaur theme. Instead of a town welcome sign, for example, Vernal has a "welcome dinosaur"—a tyrannosaurus rex, to be specific. The huge meat-eater look-alike stands alongside the road by a WELCOME TO VERNAL sign.

Across the street is a pink brontosaurus about thirty feet tall. You won't get this kind of welcome in most towns.

There is a great museum downtown with dozens of dinosaurs, even dinosaur skeletons. Vernal merchants paste little dinosaur stickers on their doors, compliments of the local chamber of commerce.

The chamber, by the way, issues free dinosaur hunting licenses. They permit you to "slay one Tyrannosaurus Rex, one Diplodocus Giganticus, two Stegosaurs, and four Pterodactyl."

The only thing I don't like about Vernal is you can't buy a Brontosaurus Burger anywhere in town. You have to drive over to Dinosaur, Colorado, for that.

And while we're on dinosaurs, is there any other thing in our culture that we are so fascinated with as children and still fascinated with as adults? What is it about these huge, prehistoric reptiles that fascinates us so?

Is it that they were so big? Is it that they roamed Earth for 125 million years? Or is it because they vanished so mysteriously?

I loved dinosaurs as a child and I love them today. Sometimes, I look at a lizard and try to imagine it a thousand times larger. I cannot look at a Gila monster or alligator without thinking of dinosaurs.

Dinosaurs are my favorite reptiles.

In Utah, even the most run-down towns have at least one beautiful building—a Church of Jesus Christ of Latter-Day Saints. Every other building can be falling apart, but the Mormon Church will be beautiful and usually fairly new.

There is something very nice about these Mormon towns, most of which are far from run-down. Most have wide streets, well-kept houses, and a nice city park. If you visit on a Sunday, everybody will be dressed in their Sunday best, either coming from or going to church. Every time I wander the back roads of Utah, the thought strikes me that traditional small-town America still exists.

I was surprised the other day to see several signs for fallout shelters. They were in the middle of nowhere along rural highways in Utah. Why? I seldom ever see these signs in cities anymore, yet here they were in land populated mostly by cows. All I could figure was that maybe under some of the farms there were missiles ready to be airmailed overseas. If one of those babies fired up accidentally, I guess it would be pretty handy to have a place to hide.

My high school English teacher had a fallout shelter under her home. She and her husband had worked on their hands and knees, scooping out every ounce of dirt. As I recall—and I could be wrong about this (but I don't think so)—they hauled out the dirt in coffee cans. It took them years to complete their shelter. They finished in the middle 1960s.

They gave me a tour once. I was seventeen at the time, and thought it was pretty neat—all one room of it. I figured it wouldn't be a bad place to spend a little time with my girlfriend. We'd get to know each other in ways we never knew before.

I couldn't figure out one thing, though. The shelter was right under my teacher's house. It seemed to me that after a missile hit, the house would come tumbling down—right on top of the shelter. How would my teacher and her husband get out? Still, I liked the place.

I went to a high school baseball game in Monroe yesterday. The undefeated home team, named the Rams, played a team named the Hawks, which had a 6–3 record. The Rams won, but the visiting Hawks were tough. It was the last game of the season before the playoffs, so the Rams had a ceremony after the game with their parents. Each player gave a flower to his mom, and the coach thanked the dads for their volunteer help.

One thing that surprised me was that it appeared that each of the players was still being raised by his real mother and father. In a big city, such a ceremony would be attended by many single moms. My guess is that in Utah families are stronger—perhaps because so many of these people are Mormons, who believe strongly in the institution of families. It was a nice scene.

It had been a few years since I had been to a high school sports event. One thing I noticed was how grown-up all the girls looked. A few were beautiful. My eyes kept drifting in their direction, but it was not in lust. They reminded me of when I was in high school. One girl looked very much like a girl I once puppy-loved. So I reminisced.

I remembered that young love was wonderful, yet painful at times. Falling in love then was a wonderful sensation I have not experienced so strongly since. Being jilted was so painful it could make me sick.

I recalled that the first eighteen years of my life went by as if in slow motion. Eighteen years was an eternity. The years since have flown by. It is the difference between a Piper Cub and a jet fighter.

I figured that to those young girls I was an old man, the age of their parents—a bloody fossil. Twenty years ago, I could have approached one of them and asked, "Excuse me, but would you like to accompany me to the malt shop?" Now, asking their moms

191

would be more like it. To be honest, I've been eyeing a few grand-mothers lately.

But the thing I realized most was that I was thankful to be my own age. I would never want to be a teenager again. The process of evolving from a child to an adult was the hardest work I've ever done. It would kill me to exert that kind of energy now. I like being middle-aged. It's a groovy kinda thing.

A fellow is running the generator in his fifth-wheel trailer in the campsite across from mine in Bryce Canyon National Park. Just a few minutes ago, he came outside, opened a compartment, and removed a vacuum cleaner. I guess by now he or his partner is cleaning their rug.

I don't think vacuuming a rug is a proper activity in a national park, unless you can do it in silence. The sound of the generator upsets the calm. A national park is supposed to be a place where you can come and be with nature. Generators are not natural.

I don't think generators, bug zappers, or assault rifles should be allowed in national parks.

Most of the foreign visitors at Bryce Canyon National Park seem to be Germans, but there are a few Japanese. I wonder how the Japanese feel as they look around and see us Americans with our Japanese cars, stereos, cameras, and camcorders.

Except for the RVs in the parking lot here at Sunset Overlook, at least half the vehicles are Japanese. A few minutes ago when I was at the overlook, there were probably thirty people with either 35mm cameras or video camcorders. I bet twenty-nine of those thirty cameras were Japanese-made. The Japanese visiting here must marvel at how much stuff they've sold to Americans.

A tour bus full of young Japanese people pulled into the Sunset Overlook a few minutes ago, and now about ten of the passengers are taking turns photographing each other in front of the rest rooms. I can't figure out what's so great about a picture of yourself in front of a john, when the beautiful overlook is nearby. I once used a rest room at the airport in Tokyo. It looked and worked like an American rest room. So what was the big deal about the bathroom at the overlook?

* * *

For a few years I dabbled in the public relations business. One of the most important events to a publicist is a press conference. The idea is to get a large turnout of media people. The best way to measure success is to count the television minicams.

Today, at the Sunset Overlook at Bryce, it was like a press conference. Everywhere I looked, people were using their camcorders. They were taping the scenery, little Jason and Jennifer, the chipmunks, and other tourists—including me.

I was thinking that by the time I return home, I will have appeared in several dozen home videos. Maybe I should sell ad space on my T-shirts.

I've been conducting some surveys. The results are in, and they are pretty interesting.

First, I've determined that half of all cars in the West have at least one bumper sticker. One in three has more than one bumper sticker. The most popular ones advertise radio stations. Another favorite is WE'RE SPENDING OUR CHILDREN'S INHERITANCE (popular on motor homes). Thankfully, the BABY ON BOARD stickers are gone.

My other survey has been of T-shirt wearers: 70 percent of all T-shirts have some sort of advertisement; 25 percent have an interesting piece of art; only 5 percent are plain.

Many T-shirts advertise places. I have one that says MAUI on it, but I have never been there. The shirt was a gift. One time a person asked me about it. I said I had never been there. I should have lied so the person wouldn't be disappointed. We wear these "location" T-shirts for two reasons: to brag that we've actually been somewhere; or to trick people into thinking we've been there.

I proudly wear a T-shirt from the Writer's Bar in the Raffles Hotel in Singapore. I actually had a drink there. But in two years of wearing the shirt, not one person has asked me about it. What a disappointment—I travel halfway around the world and nobody cares.

We wear shirts advertising beer. Kids wear these shirts to school even though they're too young to drink legally. Many T-shirts advertise sporting events. Runners have closets full of shirts from 10-K races and marathons.

Most of these shirts have corporate logos printed all over the back, making the shirts unattractive. But the runners wear them to show where they've raced. Other people who have never raced in their lives wear the shirts, but want people to think they have. You can tell these people because they are often fat.

Three Navajo women were selling jewelry in front of Ramsey's Shell station in Mount Carmel Junction when I stopped for gas and a new tire. I thought of checking their stuff, but I didn't. I cannot tell quality material from junk. The part of my brain that would help me do this never developed. There is only a hollow space. Those women could be selling ten-dollar bracelets they bought at a dime store for forty-nine cents. I wouldn't know the difference. They probably weren't, but I would never know. So when it comes to souvenir stands, I usually stop only to look. The only thing that I am really good at judging are jackalopes. I'm an expert on jackalopes.

I am writing today because what I wrote last night went to Word Heaven. I stayed up late writing like crazy, and was very happy that the words were coming. Then, at one o'clock I went to bed.

When I sat down at the keyboard this morning, the words were gone—disappeared from the face of the computer and even from Earth itself. Where they went, I do not know. I was one upset journalist. I don't know how I managed to lose those particular words. But lose them I did. If you find them, let me know. There's a ten-dollar reward.

In the winter, the motor home can seem so tiny. The doors are always closed to keep the heat in, and after a while the walls begin to close in.

So it is terrific here tonight in warm Zion National Park to have my door wide open. My little home seems ten times its winter size. The sound is nice too. Crickets are chirping, and if I listen carefully I can hear five deer that are grazing nearby. In the distance I can hear a woman laughing. I can smell the smoke of somebody's campfire.

The only negative thing about tonight is that the single woman camped next to me, whom I was hoping to lure into my campsite with some generic beer, was just joined by what appears to be her husband.

I should have known it was too good to be true—a single woman camped next door.

I've got to stop typing. The "no-seeum" bugs have invaded my porta-home here in Zion National Park and they are driving me nuts. I hate these microflies. They can slip in between the spaces in the screen door and the screens on the windows. They are so small, you could squash a thousand of them with one push of your baby finger. They're a pain in the you-know-what.

Right now they are after my fluorescent light—like it's a treasure. How thrilling, huh? What a life! I never want to be reincarnated as one of these flies. I'd rather be a cow.

One reason I never want to come back as a fly is they don't live very long. Some live only a couple of weeks—not even long enough to watch a miniseries.

If you are born a fly, this is how your life goes: You are a child for a day, then an adolescent the next day. The third day you feel your hormones, so you start looking for a mate. The fourth day you find one, mate, and then fly your own way. The fifth day you just eat and search for light bulbs at night. The sixth day you run into your fully grown kids. The seventh day you realize half your life has passed. You ask yourself, *What have I accomplished?*

Days eight through eleven are spent searching for food and light bulbs. Day twelve you start feeling bad. Day thirteen you can barely fly and your memory is shot. Day fourteen you die.

No, I don't want to come back as a fly. I want to come back as a rich, handsome, TV anchorperson with a beautiful wife and great kids. That's my idea of reincarnation.

Robert Ramsey was changing my tire earlier today at his dad's service station in Mount Carmel Junction. I had just made my way south on U.S. 89 after spending the morning hiking in Bryce Canyon. While I was there, I met—or at least said hello to—about seventy-five people. Of those, fifty were German.

"Do you get a lot of Germans here?" I asked Robert as he prepared to hoist up the front of the Dodge. "I'd say about seventy-five percent of our business is foreigners, probably sixty percent from Europe, Germans mostly," he answered.

The Germans, it seems, have invaded the West. Their assault vehicles are tour buses, Winnebagos, and other porta-homes. Their mission, in most cases, is to see the West in ten to fourteen days.

If you ask them what they think of the West, 90 percent of them will answer in four words: "It is so big."

A big lizard just darted across the campground road here in Zion National Park. It's spring, but already this morning it must be 75 degrees.

After freezing for the winter, the lizards around here must be in heaven. With the warmer weather they can move at lightning speed. In the cold they can't move at all.

What a great feeling it must be to suddenly go from paralyzed to energized. If reptiles could whistle, the lizards of Zion would be whistling a happy tune.

We humans are lucky we are not reptiles. A reptile does fine in the hot summer, but not in the winter. He's useless when the temperature dips below about sixty. Believe it or not, some scientists say we could have evolved from reptiles if things had worked out a little differently way back when.

If we had evolved from reptiles, people living in the tropics would rule the world. The Russians would be wimps, because they'd be frozen up eight months out of twelve. In the United States, you'd be relatively OK if you lived in Florida or southern California.

Dating would be tough. If you made a date with a nice woman and then it got very cold, you might show up late. She'd be mad, so you'd probably end up arguing all evening in front of an electric heater. The term *heated conversation* would take on a new meaning.

Nobody would snow ski, but water skiing on Arizona's Lake Powell would be popular. Power failures would be disastrous, especially for people sleeping with electric blankets. They'd be frozen until the power returned. If it never did, they'd be bedridden until spring.

Perhaps the worst thing about being a reptile would be that

we'd have scales. While that doesn't sound very attractive, the phrase "Boy, she has great scales" would become popular at the beach.

With rare exceptions, people in campgrounds are honest. For example, today in Zion National Park, tenters have gone off to hike, leaving their ice chests, lawn chairs, and Coleman lanterns for anyone to take. Yet, when these campers return tonight, chances are 99.9 percent that their equipment will still be there.

At home, these people would never even leave their homes unlocked, much less leave something valuable in their front yard for someone to steal. Yet out here they are trusting. It's nice to know there is still a place where people still think they can trust one another.

So far on my current trip, I have seen ten cows for every human. I have seen four sheep for every human. I have seen two antelope for every human. I have seen at least a hundred fifty COW ON ROAD warning signs, and at least fifty of the beasts actually on the pavement. Today, forced to travel thirty-five miles of Interstate, I saw a car with a California license plate. I can't recall seeing another California plate for at least a week.

Tonight I am camped in the Butch Cassidy Campground in Salina. Across the street is the Don Ho Cafe. I asked the campground manager if I had somehow been magically transported to Hawaii, where the famous singer Don Ho hangs out. She told me that I am indeed in Salina, Utah, and that Don Ho's is a good place to get Chinese food.

Driving from the south on U.S. Highway 191, fifteen minutes shy of Moab, you turn a corner to a view of twenty-foot-high white letters painted on the side on a red rock cliff: HOLE 'N THE ROCK. Right below those huge letters, next to the huge parking lot, is one of the strangest houses in the whole U.S. of A.

It's built right into the side of a solid wall of sandstone rock. Albert Christensen blasted and drilled for twelve years, then in 1952 built a home for himself and his wife, Gladys, inside the huge hole. Albert died of a heart attack in 1957. Gladys lived another seventeen years, operating a gift shop and showing curious folks around for a price. Today, about forty thousand people a year visit the cave home—the kind of place Batman would kill for.

The house Albert built is five thousand square feet—one huge cavern divided by three rock pillars. There are fourteen rooms furnished as they were when Albert and Gladys inhabited the place. There are even two stuffed horses and a stuffed donkey named Harry—a sorry sight, I'm sad to report. The poor animal has a zipperlike stitch from his chest to neck; he looks like an early experiment in bypass surgery. But there's another explanation. "Harry was Albert's pet and his first taxidermy project," said my guide, Dawn Malich.

Visitors react differently to the cave house. "Boy, this place is neat," said a little boy on my tour. He said, "Boy, this is neat" again as he peered in the cavernous bathroom. Later, I overheard two women getting ready to drive off. "I wouldn't give 'em a nickle for that place," one said.

Personally, I liked it. You'd never have to reshingle the roof— and if the enemy ever decided to nuke Utah, you could survive the blast.

My ten-minute tour was $1.60—sixteen cents a minute, I calculated, which isn't bad considering Albert spent twelve years building the place.

Albert's stepson Hub Davis runs the tourist attraction these days. He and his wife have a home in Moab, but they sleep in the cave house as well.

"People wake you up at all hours of the night," complained Davis. "They even steal the cactus. I got a letter from a lady once who said she stole a piece of cactus from me a year before and now it had died; she asked me if I'd send her another one." He laughed. "I did it. I sent her another one."

When is the last time you screamed? Screaming is like running or riding a bicycle. If you haven't done it in a long time, it's fun. If you haven't run for a while, stop reading and go outside right now and run about fifty yards. It's a great feeling—one of freedom. It's the same with riding a bicycle. When you haven't ridden one for a year or more, it feels terrific to hop on and pedal around. Coasting is especially fun, because it feels so smooth as you move along without any effort.

Screaming is even better. But, realistically, you can't go around screaming in the city. People will hear you. They'll get upset. They'll call the cops. And face it: A quiet scream is not satisfying. Kids can scream in the city, and that's one good reason never to grow up.

I screamed recently. And I'm here to tell you I can hardly wait to do it again. I was on a dirt road outside of Moab in the middle of nowhere, there was nobody else around, and I was stopped on a ridge overlooking maybe a hundred square miles of the most beautiful red-rock country in the world. As I stood there, I was happy but a little dissatisfied. Something was missing. Then I had the answer. I needed to express the wonderful feelings all bottled up inside of me. There was only one way: I needed to scream.

It was a foreign idea, for I had not screamed in years except at a few NBA games when ten thousand other people were also screaming, so I couldn't even hear my own noise.

So there near Moab, I stood up and looked over the huge area below me, took a deep breath, and then I proceeded to scream. But it was a timid scream and unsatisfying. I was out of practice. So I screamed again, this time louder. It felt better.

Then, feeling a huge urge inside me, I drew all the air I could into my lungs, paused for a second to let it settle in real well, and then looked out over that valley before me, stood as tall as I could stand, and proceeded to let out the loudest scream I had ever screamed in my forty-plus years on this planet. It was a "blood-curdling scream" for sure.

It was great! In fact it was so great, I have now amended my list of hobbies: golf, tennis, hiking, writing, photography—and screaming.

I love the red country around Moab. When I want to imagine what heaven is like, I think of a sunny spring day in Moab. Yesterday, hiking in Arches National Park—which is only a short drive from town—I felt a million miles from anything unpleasant. Everything was beautiful, and my every move felt in slow motion. I thought to myself that when God created Earth, he spent extra time here—like it was a pet project. I wondered how any place could be so gorgeous.

Tears came to my eyes as I stood before a huge arch in the sandstone rock. It was that beautiful. I was reminded of how precious it is to be alive..

That night, I slept with a smile on my face. I'm sure of it.

CHAPTER EIGHT

GOING HOME

THERE comes a time on each of my trips when I must go home to Sacramento. An alarm sounds in my head and it can only be silenced by the sight of my driveway.

It is as if that alarm activates a huge magnet back home that locks directly on me—whether I'm in Colorado, Washington, New Mexico—anywhere. I will hear, "It is time, Chuck, to go home," and then I will feel a force pulling me there. There may be back roads to roam and stories to write, but the alarm has sounded, and that is all that matters.

That afternoon when I would normally stop for the night, I still drive. Later, too tired to go on, I will study a map at my campsite for the fastest route home. Now it is time for an Interstate—a straight and fast road with fast food, fast gas, and roadside rests for fast rests.

On my last trip my dash home was insane—the force was especially strong. I drove the 750 miles from Moab to Reno in one long day, stopping for gas five times in the process—a personal record. I drank coffee and Coke and gorged myself with food from a nutritionist's nightmare—Eskimo Pies, Cheez-Its, and Snickers bars. I raced across lonely Interstate 80 at night, stopping in Wendover for gas and a cheeseburger, in Winnemucca for beef jerky, and finally in Reno for sleep.

Wells, Carlin, and Lovelock were only lighted blurs—all bypassed in my mad race with an invisible clock. It was just me and the truckers in a dark Nevada desert. A gallon of black coffee flowed in my veins, supercharging my awareness of everything: The reflectors at construction zones seemed as bright as the lights on the Las Vegas strip; the aroma of sagebrush made my nose crazy. Sometimes a truck would come from behind out of nowhere, and when he passed me, I would jump. Too much coffee, I would tell myself. Then there was that long tunnel in the desert— forgotten since my previous trips—but all lit up like Los Angeles or San Francisco. I shot through it like a man in a missile.

And always there was the road—the long, lonely, dark, and desolate road.

The truckers and I played highway leapfrog—shifting positions to avoid boredom. I'd go ahead, a truck would go ahead, and then we'd switch again. Sometimes for twenty miles, a lone eighteen-wheeler and my motor home were the only civilization.

My CB was down, so I couldn't talk. But I wondered who was in that cab ahead. Where was he headed at 1:30 A.M. in the middle of the American Outback?

Every once in a while, I'd see a light or two in the distance—a home with no neighbors. Who could live in such a place?

All the time, I was racing westbound at ninety-five feet a second—heading home on the I-80 desert expressway.

"If you've got the money, honey, I've got the time," Willie Nelson sang from my stereo. And then Linda Ronstadt would have her turn, and I'd sing along, and all the while my tires were rollin' on, and my porta-house with its shower and freezer and double bed was taking me home.

At three in the morning I parked in Reno, too exhausted to go on. My insides were still going sixty-five—the aftershock of eighteen hours on the road. Still, a minute later I was in bed and asleep.

I woke up at dawn with sand in my eyes and adrenaline in my blood. A half hour and two cups of coffee later I was moving again, up on I-80, fighting the morning rush, listening to KOH, and zooming west. The Sierra Nevada mountains were just ahead, and then I was past Boomtown and climbing toward California. WEL- COME TO CALIFORNIA, the big sign said, and I saluted as I passed. Then I flew by Truckee, then Donner Summit, and then the great and hazy valley of California was spread out before me. I dropped into it at Loomis, and a half hour later I was home.

The neighbor's cat was on the same fence he was on when I left, and he was smiling the same feline smile. I said hello, and he wagged his tail to say, "Get lost."

My innards were still speeding, but I was worn out and sleepy and my right foot was gas-pedaled out. I was experiencing caffeine withdrawal and a highway version of jet lag.

There was a stack of mail on my kitchen table, and the phone answering machine was blinking with a half dozen messages. But it didn't matter. What mattered was that I was home.

The couch mattered, too. So I took off my shoes, grabbed a pillow, and lay down.

Three hours later I woke up. The alarm clock in my head was silent, and my insides were calm. But the alarm will sound again soon—just as it had a few days earlier when it ordered me home. Except the next alarm will deliver a different message.

"Get on the road," it will say.